TRUDY HAYDEN was Director of the Privacy Project of the American Civil Liberties Union and author of ACLU "Privacy Report" from 1974 to 1978. She is presently Director of Research for the New York State Commission on the Family Court Act, and a consultant on privacy to the New York Civil Liberties Union. She also writes and lectures frequently on privacy issues.

JACK DAVID NOVIK is National Staff Counsel of the American Civil Liberties Union, Counsel to the ACLU Foundation's Project on Privacy and Data Collection and Counsel to the Project on National Security and Civil Liberties. In those capacities Mr. Novik has litigated many intelligence abuse, freedom of information and privacy cases. Mr. Novik also lectures on privacy issues and is co-author of "Litigation Under the Federal Freedom of Information Act and Privacy Acts" published by the Center for National Security Studies.

Also in this Series

THE RIGHTS OF ALIENS	44925	$1.95
THE RIGHTS OF CANDIDATES AND VOTERS	49940	$2.50
THE RIGHTS OF EX-OFFENDERS	44701	$1.95
THE RIGHTS OF GAY PEOPLE	24976	$1.75
THE RIGHTS OF GOVERNMENT EMPLOYEES	38505	$1.75
THE RIGHTS OF HOSPITAL PATIENTS	39198	$1.75
THE RIGHTS OF MENTAL PATIENTS	36574	$1.75
THE RIGHTS OF MENTALLY RETARDED PERSONS	31351	$1.50
THE RIGHTS OF MILITARY PERSONNEL	33365	$1.50
THE RIGHTS OF OLDER PERSONS	44362	$2.50
THE RIGHTS OF THE POOR	28002	$1.25
THE RIGHTS OF PRISONERS	35436	$1.50
THE RIGHTS OF PHYSICALLY HANDICAPPED PEOPLE	47274	$2.25
THE RIGHTS OF RACIAL MINORITIES	75077	$1.95
THE RIGHTS OF REPORTERS	38836	$1.75
THE RIGHTS OF STUDENTS	47019	$1.75
THE RIGHTS OF SUSPECTS	28043	$1.25
THE RIGHTS OF TEACHERS	25049	$1.50
THE RIGHTS OF VETERANS	36285	$1.75
THE RIGHTS OF UNION MEMBERS	46193	$2.25
THE RIGHTS OF WOMEN	27953	$1.75
THE RIGHTS OF YOUNG PEOPLE	42077	$1.75

Where better paperbacks are sold, or directly from the publisher.
Include 50¢ per copy for mailing; allow 4-6 weeks for delivery.

Avon Books, Mail Order Dept., 250 West 55th Street,
New York, N.Y. 10019

AN AMERICAN
CIVIL LIBERTIES
UNION HANDBOOK

YOUR RIGHTS
TO PRIVACY

THE BASIC ACLU
GUIDE FOR YOUR
RIGHTS TO PRIVACY

TRUDY HAYDEN
and
JACK NOVIK

General Editor of this series:
Norman Dorsen, *President, ACLU*

AVON
PUBLISHERS OF BARD, CAMELOT AND DISCUS BOOKS

AVON BOOKS
A division of
The Hearst Corporation
959 Eighth Avenue
New York, New York 10019

Copyright © 1980
by The American Civil Liberties Union
Published by arrangement with
The American Civil Liberties Union
Library of Congress Catalog Card Number: 80-66735
ISBN: 0-380-75895-4

First Avon Printing, August, 1980

AVON TRADEMARK REG. U.S. PAT. OFF. AND IN
OTHER COUNTRIES, MARCA REGISTRADA, HECHO EN
U.S.A.

Printed in the U.S.A.

Acknowledgments

We would like to express our appreciation to Aryeh Neier, former Executive Director of the ACLU, and John Shattuck, ACLU's Washington Office Director, for reading our manuscript and making valuable suggestions. Our thanks also to Lisa Grapek for helping us with research on state privacy laws.

Contents

Preface

This guide sets forth your rights under present law and offers suggestions on how you can protect your rights. It is one of a continuing series of handbooks published in cooperation with the American Civil Liberties Union.

The hope surrounding these publications is that Americans informed of their rights will be encouraged to exercise them. Through their exercise, rights are given life. If they are rarely used, they may be forgotten and violations may become routine.

This guide offers no assurances that your rights will be respected. The laws may change and, in some of the subjects covered in these pages, they change quite rapidly. An effort has been made to note those parts of the law where movement is taking place but it is not always possible to predict accurately when the law *will* change.

Even if the laws remain the same, interpretations of them by courts and administrative officials often vary. In a federal system such as ours, there is a built-in problem of the differences between state and federal law, not to speak of the confusion of the differences from state to state. In addition, there are wide variations in the ways in which particular courts and administrative officials will interpret the same law at any given moment.

If you encounter what you consider to be a specific abuse of your rights you should seek legal assistance. There are a number of agencies that may help you, among them ACLU affiliate offices, but bear in mind that the ACLU is a limited-purpose organization. In many communities, there are federally funded legal service offices which provide assistance to poor persons who cannot afford the costs of legal representation. In general, the rights that the ACLU defend are freedom of inquiry and expression; due process of law; equal protection of the laws; and privacy. The authors in this series have discussed other rights in these books (even though they sometimes fall outside the ACLU's usual concern) in order to provide as much guidance as possible.

These books have been planned as guides for the people directly affected: therefore the question and answer format. In some of these areas there are more detailed works available for "experts." These guides seek to raise the largest issues and inform the non-specialist of the basic laws on the subject. The authors of the books are themselves specialists who understand the need for information at "street level."

No attorney can be an expert in every part of the law. If you encounter a specific legal problem in an area discussed in one of these handbooks, show the book to your attorney. Of course, he will not be able to rely *exclusively* on the handbook to provide you with adequate representation. But if he hasn't had a great deal of experience in the specific area, the handbook can provide helpful suggestions on how to proceed.

Norman Dorsen, Chairperson
American Civil Liberties Union

The principal purpose of this handbook, and others in this series, is to inform individuals of their legal rights. The authors from time to time suggest what the law should be, but the author's personal views are not necessarily those of the ACLU. For the ACLU's position on the issues discussed in this handbook, the reader should write to Librarian, ACLU, 22 East 40th Street, New York, N.Y. 10016.

Introduction

As individuals, we all have some intuitive sense of territory which we try to protect against intruders. Although the boundaries and importance of that private domain may vary from person to person, it is generally agreed that privacy is important. Indeed, privacy is one of those fundamental principles by which we define ourselves as a people: the American creed emphasizes the preeminent importance of the individual and the very limited intrusions which are allowed the government.

Although a sense of the importance of privacy is deeply ingrained in our political and social heritage, the right of privacy is not explicitly mentioned in the Constitution. Of course, the Bill of Rights is, by its very nature, a broad affirmation of personal privacy because it strictly limits the government's power to interfere with individual liberty. And the Constitution does specifically protect some components of privacy: the free-speech and free-exercise-of-religion provisions of the First Amendment assure the privacy of personal beliefs and associations; the Fourth Amendment protects "persons, houses, papers, and effects" from unreasonable search and seizure; and the Fifth Amendment protections against self-incrimination restrain the government from coercing an individual to breach his or her own privacy.

The development of privacy as a working legal concept, however, has not equaled its importance as an article of faith. The law of privacy suffered a grudging and hesitant birth and its growth has been stunted by the entrenched resistance of opposing interests.

In part, the problem is that privacy is not a single concept but a loose amalgam of different interests difficult to combine in one formulation. The Fourth Amendment prohibition against unreasonable searches and seizures, for example, was described by Justice Brandeis as the constitutional expression of the "right to be let alone." [1] The privacy protections in the First Amendment suggest the values of personal autonomy, focusing not on what the government can do, but rather on the individual's freedom to be. Another aspect of privacy that is especially important in this age of computer technology, but one lacking specific protection in the Constitution, is the right to exercise some measure of "control over information about oneself." [2]

The emergence of a separate and distinct body of law dealing with privacy is generally credited to an influential law-review article written by Samuel Warren and Louis Brandeis in 1890.[3] However, the right to privacy which they advocated concentrated on an individual's interest in preventing the commercialization of private matters by the fast-paced and often unscrupulous press of the 1890s. Thereafter, in very cautious increments, the courts and legislatures first accepted, and then defined and enforced, a number of different principles which were described generally as a "right to privacy." [4] Intrusions on privacy were recognized as a civil wrong—in legal parlance, a tort. In some jurisdictions, it is improper for a person to publicize certain private facts about another without consent. A closely related tort is casting another in a bad public light by disseminating information reflecting an undesirable and erroneous public image of that person. Physical intrusion into a person's home or solitude, such as by eavesdropping, is also now often recognized as a tort.

The right to privacy was initially interpreted to include only protection against tangible intrusions resulting in measurable injury. Courts were accustomed to thinking in those terms and took longer to address the more difficult issues of personal autonomy and information control.

During the first half of the twentieth century, the Supreme Court began to explore the meaning and application of various constitutional principles which would later become the constituent elements, and supporting structure, of the constitutional right of privacy. In 1923 for example, the Supreme Court invalidated a state law prohibiting the teaching of any language other than English. Such a law, as the Court saw it, interfered with the rights of personal autonomy: "The right of the individual to contract, to engage in any of the common occupations of life, to acquire useful knowledge, to marry, to establish a home and bring up children, to worship God according to the dictates of . . . conscience, and, generally, to enjoy those privileges long recognized as essential to the orderly pursuit of happiness by free men. . . ." [5] Similarly, recognizing that "the fundamental theory of liberty . . . excludes any general power of the state" to compel standardization, the Court struck down a law requiring all children to attend public schools.[6] In a later decision which combined a recognition of the values of personal autonomy and information control as well as First Amendment associational privacy, the court refused to allow a state to compel the disclosure of organizational membership lists. The decision articulated the "right of the members to pursue their lawful private interest privately and to associate freely with others" without "the deterrent effect . . . which disclosure of membership lists is likely to have." [7]

In 1965, in *Griswold* v. *Connecticut*,[8] the Supreme Court held that the Constitution included an implied right of privacy. The case involved a Connecticut statute prohibiting even married people from using contraceptives. Justice Douglas, writing for the Court, said that a "zone of privacy" within a "penumbra" was created by several fundamental constitutional guarantees, including the First, Fourth, and Fifth Amendments. Although they agreed on the result, the majority Justices could not agree on the philosophical underpinnings of the constitutional right of privacy, and the theoretical basis for the right is still debated among legal scholars.

The Court's decision in *Griswold* was influenced strongly by the Justices' "notions of privacy surrounding the marriage relationship." Subsequent to 1965, the Court has expanded somewhat its application of the concept of privacy in dealing with marital or sexual issues. For example, in *Eisenstadt* v. *Baird*,[9] the Court built on the *Griswold* precedent to protect the right to distribute contraceptives to unmarried people: "If the right of privacy means anything, it is the right of the *individual*, married or single, to be free from unwarranted governmental intrusion into matters so fundamentally affecting a person as the decision whether to bear or beget a child." In *Roe* v.

Wade,[10] the right of privacy was held to include a woman's right to choose to have an abortion. The Court has also ruled that the right of privacy, coupled with First Amendment protections for freedom of speech and the press, invalidated a state law prohibiting the possession of obscene materials in a person's own home for personal use.[11]

The *Griswold* decision offered hope that the newly articulated right of privacy would develop so as to protect the individual against the sophisticated intrusions of modern technology and the insistent prying of government. Those hopes have not been realized. In recent years, the Supreme Court has steadfastly refused to provide such constitutional protection for the right to privacy.

In the early marital-sexual cases the Justices were influenced by their own notions of decency, which did not permit the government to take an interest in what people did in their bedrooms. In other cases the Court has refused to allow privacy claims to take precedence over competing interests of government, especially law enforcement. For example, the Court upheld the validity of the Bank Secrecy Act, enacted to combat white-collar crime, even though the law allowed government virtually unlimited access to an individual's bank records.[12] The Court's insensitivity to concern about information collection is strikingly demonstrated by its conclusion that depositors have no "legitimate expectation of privacy" in their bank records.

The Court has shown a similar disregard for the privacy of medical records by upholding a New York law requiring that copies of all prescriptions for narcotics be forwarded to the state capital for storage and computerization.[13] And the Court dismissed a case against a local police department which misused an arrest record. In that case, the police circulated the name and picture of a man identified as a known shoplifter even though the charges had been dismissed.[14]

As briefly summarized above, privacy interests first developed in the context of specific constitutional provisions which made no mention of privacy—First Amendment freedom of speech, religion, and association; Fourth Amendment freedom from arbitrary seizures and intrusions; Fifth Amendment freedom of due process. The Supreme Court then explicitly articulated an implied right of privacy; but the Court has refused to expand that concept much beyond its very limited origins. Therefore in recent years current constitutional privacy interests are once again being considered in the context of the specific underlying constitutional rights which form the component elements of privacy. For example, the government's abusive intelligence operations—including political surveillance, counterintelligence operations, wiretapping, etc.—are all being challenged as First Amendment violations. Similarly the due-process rights of the Fifth and Fourteenth Amendments are established checks on the government's power to interfere with personal autonomy. On the other hand, many Fourth Amendment protections have been sacrificed to competing government (especially law-enforcement)interests and, as a result, the Fourth Amendment is now a crumbling bastion of "the right of the people to be secure in their persons, houses, papers, and effects." Thus, the constitutional law of privacy is presently a diffuse amalgam of related constitutional issues which have not yet gelled into a comprehensive, unitary theory of privacy.

During the past decade, in which the Supreme Court has been struggling with the substance and dimensions of constitutional privacy, the Congress has also considered privacy. Proponents of privacy have introduced legislation addressing virtually every privacy issue. Although only few protections have been enacted, the proposals have resulted in lengthy congressional investigations and a heightened public awareness of the stakes involved. Some important laws that have been adopted include the Privacy Act and the Freedom of Information Act (concerning personal records maintained by the federal government),[15] the Fair Credit Reporting Act (credit records),[16] and the Buckley Amendment (school records).[17]

"Privacy" can be defined to embrace virtually every point at which the individual and the world interact. But this book focuses principally on the privacy of information. In today's technological society, information is power and dissemination of information affords the government and business power to intrude in and control our lives. Accordingly, the unrestrained maintenance and misuse of informational files—dossiers—is a serious threat to privacy. This book details some of the problems associated with different kinds of records and a variety of record-collecting practices. Obviously, consideration of all the ramifications of information privacy is beyond the scope of this book. We have therefore focused on the most pressing information-privacy problems confronting people every day; the emphasis is on general principles which have broad application.

The book is divided into three parts: the privacy of personal records, intrusion into personal thoughts, and the control of government information about the individual. Not surprisingly, lines between those areas are indistinct and the issues often overlap.

Although this Introduction has focused on the development of federal law, the states have also been attentive to privacy concerns. Some have adopted progressive and far-reaching laws. Several states now have their own constitutional provisions explicitly protecting the right of privacy, and many states have enacted laws protecting privacy. Because the substance of state privacy laws nationwide changes rapidly, anyone with a particular privacy problem will need to go further in determining what state laws are applicable.[18]

NOTES

1. Olmstead v. United States, 277 U.S. 438, 478 (1928) (Brandeis, J. dissenting).
2. A. WESTIN, *Privacy and Freedom* 32 (Atheneum 1967).
3. Warren and Brandeis, *The Right to Privacy*, 4 HARV. L. REV. 193 (1890).
4. See, generally, PROSSER, *Law of Torts* 829 *et seq.* (3rd ed. 1964).
5. Meyer v. Nebraska, 262 U.S. 390 (1923).
6. Pierce v. Society of Sisters, 268 U.S. 510 (1925).
7. NAACP v. Alabama, 357 U.S. 449, 466 (1958).
8. 381 U.S. 479 (1965).
9. 405 U.S. 438 (1972).
10. 410 U.S. 113 (1973).
11. Stanley v. Georgia, 394 U.S. 557 (1969).
12. United States v. Miller, 425 U.S. 435 (1976).
13. Whalen v. Roe, 429 U.S. 589 (1977).
14. Paul v. Davis, 424 U.S. 693 (1976).
15. Privacy Act, 5 U.S.C. §552a; Freedom of Information Act, 5 U.S.C. §552.

16. 15 U.S.C. §1681 *et seq.*
17. 20 U.S.C. §1232g.
18. Privacy laws vary greatly from state to state. In many instances, state law references are mentioned in the text. Any person desiring more information about laws affecting a particular privacy interest—such as credit records, polygraphs, electronic surveillance—can write to the state Attorney General's office for assistance. In most states the Attorney General will advise whether any such laws exist and, if so, provide the applicable citations. In addition, the local ACLU affiliate may be able to provide the information sought or suggest other avenues of assistance.

PART ONE
Privacy of Personal Records

I

Fairness and Consent

Are there any rules governing the maintenance of personal-record systems?

Yes. *Fair information practices* are standards governing the maintenance of personal-record systems which allow people to exercise some control over their own records.

The basic principles of fair information practice are:

1. All personal-record systems must be a matter of public knowledge; there must be no personal-record system whose existence is secret.
2. Individuals must be able to examine, copy, and correct their own records.
3. Individuals must be able to find out how information about them is used and who has access to it.
4. Information obtained for one purpose may not be used or made available for any other purpose without the individual's consent.
5. Any agency or organization that collects, maintains, uses, or disseminates personally identifiable records is responsible for the timeliness, accuracy, completeness, and relevance of the records and for protecting against their improper use or disclosure.
6. Individuals must have legal recourse to enforce their "expectation of confidentiality" and their other rights of fair information practice.

Are fair information practices enforced by law?

Yes. Codes of fair information practice form the basic structure of most record-privacy statutes. The federal Privacy Act of 1974 imposes a code of fair information practice upon federal agencies that maintain personal-record systems.[1] (Federal-agency information practices are described in detail in Chapter XII.) A few states have passed

3

their own privacy acts imposing general codes of fair
information practice on state (and in some cases, local)
government personal-record systems.² The Family Educational Rights and Privacy Act, a federal statute governing
student records, contains a code of fair information practice.³ So too, in a more limited way, does the federal Fair
Credit Reporting Act, dealing with credit records.⁴ Other
statutes contain at least some elements of a code of fair
information practices—for example, the federal and state
Freedom of Information Acts, under which individuals
can obtain access to their own records, and federal and
state bank-privacy statutes, which protect individuals
against unauthorized disclosures of their bank records.

A principal object of current efforts to enact record-
privacy legislation both in Congress and in the state legislatures is to establish codes of fair information practice
applicable to all personal-record systems, whether they
are maintained by government agencies or by private institutions.

Must individuals be asked for their consent before personal information can be collected or disseminated?

Individual *consent* is frequently assumed to be a prerequisite to the collection, use, and dissemination of information about a particular person. The record subject's
consent is presumed to legitimize the record-keeper's collection and use of personal data. The principle of consent
assumes two conditions: that consent is informed, and that
it is freely given. But in practice, these assumptions are
not borne out. Individuals usually have only the vaguest
idea what information will be collected, how it will be
used, or where it will be disseminated, and their consent
is usually elicited in circumstances that leave them no
effective opportunity to refuse.

In succeeding chapters the problem of the "blanket
waiver" will be discussed. This is the way most people are
asked for their consent to the collection, use, or dissemination of personal data. It may be an authorization to an
insurance company to obtain medical records, or to a
prospective employer to investigate an applicant's background and reputation. The person has no way of knowing
exactly what records or data are sought or from whom,
no way of restricting or even tracing their dissemination,

no way of limiting the duration or scope of the authorization. Most institutions simply refuse to deal with a person unless he signs a waiver, so that the "consent" is a requirement for whatever benefit or service is involved—a job, an insurance policy, medical care, welfare benefits.

Privacy advocates are seeking the enactment of codes of fair information practice that will address these problems of consent. They believe that an agency or institution that gathers, uses, or disseminates information about a person must tell him, in precise and specific language, exactly what records are to be disclosed or obtained, where they are, who will see them, and for what purposes they will be used; that all consent forms must include an expiration date; and that all record-keepers must inform individuals, in precise and specific language, what kinds of records or information might be obtained or disseminated without their explicit prior consent.

Even such stringent notification requirements, however, would still leave the problem of coercion. Thus, some privacy advocates suggest that the word "consent," with its implications of permission freely granted, be abandoned, and that the word "authorization" be adopted in its stead.[5]

NOTES

1. 5 U.S.C. 552a.
2. See ARK. STAT. ANN. §§16–802 et seq.; CAL. CIV. CODE §§1798 et seq.; CONN. GEN. STAT. ANN. §§4–190 et seq.; IND. STAT. ANN. §4–1–6; MASS. ANN. LAWS ch. 30, §63, ch. 66A, §§1–3, ch. 214, §3B; MINN. STAT. ANN. §§15.162 et seq.; OHIO REV. CODE ANN. §§1347.01 et seq.; UTAH CODE ANN. §§63–50–1 et seq.; VA. CODE §§2.1–377 et seq.
3. 20 U.S.C. 1232g.
4. 15 U.S.C. 1681 et seq.
5. Privacy Protection Study Commission, Personal Privacy in an Information Society 19 (U.S. Government Printing Office, July 1977).

II

School Records

What kinds of information are contained in school records?

Much more than just grades. School records describe students' emotional development, social behavior, medical problems, learning problems, political and religious preferences, family members, physical appearance, hobbies and extracurricular interests, ethnic background, economic circumstances, attitudes toward teachers and other students, psychological test scores, criminal history, even personal secrets confided to a friendly teacher or counselor. Their contents range from such objective information as a student's height and weight to the subjective impressions of a teacher about the "tendencies" of an unruly child.

Many people attend school from the time they are three or four years old until their mid-twenties and even beyond. Records generated by each school experience follow the student into subsequent classes and schools, and they are likely to determine how the student is evaluated and placed by every new teacher and institution in turn. The records maintained on a kindergarten child may someday have an effect on his admission to college or acceptance for employment. Because school records are so influential, and so long-lived, it is important that parents and students know what they contain, and who has access to them.

Do students have a right to see their own school records?

Yes, if a student is either eighteen years old or attends college, university, or other postsecondary institution, and if the school he attends receives any federal money from the U.S. Office of Education. Such a student's right of access is provided by a federal statute enacted in 1974, the Family Educational Rights and Privacy Act (FERPA), known also as the Buckley Amendment.[1] In some localities state laws, formal state or local school-board policies, or the administrative policies of individual schools may give students under eighteen a right of access to some or all of their own education records.

The rights of access and other rights conferred by FERPA do not apply to students at private institutions. Nor do they apply to students at schools receiving all kinds of federal aid. Only schools that get federal funds through a program administered by the U.S. Commissioner of Education are obligated to comply with FERPA. A list of such programs is published each year, and can be obtained from any regional office of the U.S. Department of Education. The designated programs include some that make loans and grants directly to students which are then paid to the school for educational services.[2]

Do parents have a right to see their children's school records?

Yes. If a student is under eighteen and attends an elementary or secondary school that receives U.S. Office of Education funds, FERPA gives his parents the right of access to his records. When the student becomes an "eligible student" within the definition of the statute—turns eighteen, or enters a postsecondary educational institution—rights of access and other rights under FERPA are automatically transferred from the parents to the student.

Do students have a right to see records maintained by schools they no longer attend?

Yes. But FERPA rights of access do not cover a person who applied for admission but was not accepted.[3] A person turned down for admission to a college does not have a statutory right to see the material in his admission file, and so may not be able to learn why he was rejected.

How do students and parents know what kinds of records are being kept?

Each school subject to FERPA must make available to parents and students, on request, a listing of the types and locations of the personal-record systems it maintains, together with the titles and addresses of the officials responsible for each system of records.[4]

Do students and their parents have the right to see all of their records?

No. Some records may be withheld.

FERPA rights of access do not cover so-called "desk-drawer notes," the informal notes about students kept by teachers and other school personnel solely for their own use, so long as these are not accessible or revealed to any other person except an official substitute teacher or administrator. Nor do they cover records kept by a campus security force, provided that: (1) such records are separately maintained and used only for law-enforcement purposes; (2) they are not disclosed to anyone except law-enforcement officials in the same jurisdiction (e.g., the local police); and (3) the school's security personnel do not have access to the student's other school records.[5]

Students who are eighteen years or older, or who attend a college or other postsecondary institution, do not have a right of direct access to medical or psychiatric records, so long as these were created and maintained solely for treatment purposes and are not disclosed to anyone other than individuals providing treatment. These records may, however, be released to a physician of the student's choice—who is then free, of course, to show them to the student. Such records are available to the parents of elementary and secondary students under eighteen.[6]

FERPA rights of access do not allow postsecondary students to see their parents' financial statements, such as statements submitted in applications for scholarship aid. They do not allow students to see confidential letters of recommendation filed before January 1, 1975, so long as these are used only for their originally intended purpose. (If a letter filed before that date, originally used for college admission, is later used for another purpose, such as employment, the student may see it.) And finally, students may not have access to letters of recommendation filed after January 1, 1975, with respect to which they have formally waived their rights of access.[7]

How—and why—do students waive their rights of access to confidential letters of recommendation?

In its original form, FERPA would have allowed eligible students or parents to see all letters of recommendation written on their behalf by teachers and others for use in applications for college or graduate-school admission, fellowships, special educational programs, employment, etc. The prospect that these traditionally secret letters would be revealed to students so alarmed some professional educators that they lobbied to have the law amended. Advocates on the other side argued that because these letters are so influential in making decisions, particularly for college and graduate-school admissions, and because they frequently contain derogatory, misleading, or altogether false information, it was essential that students retain the right to see them. Congress compromised, amending the law to preserve the confidentiality of letters filed before January 1, 1975, and to allow a voluntary waiver of the student's right of access to letters filed after that date.

A waiver of the right of access must be executed in writing. It must be signed by an eligible student or by a parent—unless the student is an applicant for admission to a postsecondary institution, in which case he must execute the waiver himself, even if he is under eighteen. An educational institution may not require a waiver as a condition of admission, financial aid, or any service or benefit. The student must be given, on request, the name of every person who provides a confidential letter. A waiver is valid only so long as a letter of recommendation is used for its originally intended purpose: admission to an educational institution, employment, or the receipt of an honor or honorary recognition. It may be revoked at any time, with respect to new uses of a letter already filed or new letters filed after the date of revocation, and an eligible student may revoke a waiver previously executed by his parent. The waiver must specify the categories of records to which it applies and their intended uses: the student may not be asked to sign a blanket waiver of all his rights of access.[8]

Despite these apparently rigorous safeguards, the waiver provision is one of the most commonly abused sections of FERPA. There have been reports of blatant coercion:

e.g., the high-school guidance counselor who refuses to process any college application unless the student signs a waive. More frequent, though, is the subtle coercion imposed by the advice given to students that their college applications will not be seriously considered unless they waiver their right to see letters of recommendation. Some college and graduate-school administrators have perpetuated the tradition of secrecy by insisting that only confidential letters can be "frank," and many application forms contain a bland statement instructing the student to "sign below to waive your right of access to letters of recommendation."

It is very difficult for an individual to withstand this kind of pressure. Unless the law is changed, or until the academic community changes its own thinking, students may be pushed into signing waivers against their own better judgment. But it should always be remembered that an institution cannot *require* a waiver, and the student is always within his rights to refuse.

How do students and parents get to see school records?

Each institution is allowed to set its own procedures for the inspection of records. FERPA requires that the school notify students and parents annually about their rights under FERPA and about the procedures to be followed for inspecting records. (Elementary and secondary schools must "provide for the need to effectively notify parents of students identified as having a primary or home language other than English.")[9] Occasionally, this is done by mail; more often, by notice on a bulletin board or publication in a student handbook or newspaper; but frequently, not at all.

The institution must comply with a request for access "within a reasonable period of time," but no more than forty-five days.[10] It must respond to a "reasonable" request for an explanation or interpretation of the material in the record.[11] It may not forbid the eligible student or parent to read the record or to take notes. If a record contains information on students other than the one requesting access, the institution may remove or segregate that information, but where this cannot practically be done, the pertinent parts of the record may be read to the student or parent orally. No fees may be charged to search for or retrieve a student's records.[12]

In some institutions, it may be possible for the student to inspect all of his records at once, especially if his advance notice has allowed school officials to gather the records in one place. But the law does not require this, and the student may have to visit several different offices and follow different procedures. Educational institutions have been notably lax about publishing, or even formulating, procedures for inspecting records, a failure that may cause much delay and confusion.

It is important to make a note of everything that happens in the course of attempting to examine one's school records: the date of the request for access, the date of the school's response, the date the records were examined, what records were seen, what records were withheld and the school's reasons for withholding them, any misinformation found in the records, and the names of the officials who handled each step of the process. These facts can be significant in any subsequent enforcement proceedings.

May students and parents obtain copies of records?

Yes, if the inability to obtain copies would effectively deprive them of their rights of access.[13]

There are at least two circumstances in which the right to obtain copies could be crucial. The first is inaccessibility: when a former student is far away from the institution, or a working parent is unable to make a personal visit during school hours. The second is unwieldiness: when the records are so copious or complex that visual inspection or even taking notes is not sufficient. In either circumstance, the institution must provide copies. In practice, many institutions make copies simply on request.

The institution may charge for copies, but only if the fee would not "effectively prevent the parents and students from exercising their right to inspect and review" the records.[14] This suggests that fees may have to be waived altogether for poor families, or reduced where it is necessary for the student to obtain large quantities of documents. Each institution must have a published schedule of fees for copies, available to parents and students on request.[15]

If a record contains inaccurate information, can it be changed?

Yes.

A parent or eligible student may ask the school to amend any information on the grounds that it is inaccurate, is misleading, or violates the student's right of privacy or other rights. Within a reasonable period, the institution must decide whether or not to comply. If it refuses, it must inform the parent or student of his right to a hearing.[16]

The scope of the right to challenge inaccurate or misleading information, or information that violates the student's rights, is only vaguely defined. The legislative history of FERPA is clear on at least one point: the provision is not applicable to a student's grades.[17] A student may not use FERPA to challenge the teacher's judgment in deciding what grade to give for a course. However, a student may challenge the accuracy of the record in reporting the grade actually received—e.g., if the record shows a B, whereas he actually received an A.

There are no generally accepted standards for determining what kinds of information would violate a student's privacy or other rights. FERPA itself addresses only the procedures by which an educational institution maintains and disseminates student records; it does not deal with the substantive content of the records. The student or parent who wants to challenge information on the grounds that it violates a student's rights will have to look to other statutes, regulations, and standards. He might argue, for example, that information about an arrest on charges later dismissed is confidential under a state law dealing with arrest records, or that the notation of anonymous, unsubstantiated charges of cheating or stealing violates his rights of due process, or that disparaging comments on his physical appearance are based on racially discriminatory judgments. In each instance the challenge must be shaped by the nature of the information, the kind of record in which it is contained, and the probable past and future uses of that record in making decisions about the student.

A request to amend a record should be made in writing and addressed to the principal, dean, or other designated administrative official. If the request is denied, or if no answer is given within a reasonable time, or if the institution's informal attempts to reconcile the disagreement seem to be no more than a delaying tactic, a written request for a hearing should be submitted. The "reasonable period" allotted to the institution for its reply to a request for the amendment of a record is not specified in this section of the law, although elsewhere a "reasonable period" is defined as no more than forty-five days.

Students and parents should make a note of everything that happens when they ask to have a record corrected: the date of the request, the date of the school's reply, the date of the request for a hearing, the hearing date, the names of the hearing officers, and the date and nature of the outcome. It may be necessary to use this information in a later enforcement action.

How is a hearing conducted?

Under FERPA, each educational institution is free to formulate its own procedures for conducting a hearing on a challenge to information in a record, so long as it meets the following requirements:

1. The hearing must be held within a reasonable period after the request is filed.
2. The eligible student or parent must be given reasonable advance notice of the date, time, and place of the hearing. These must be reasonably convenient for the complainant.
3. Although the hearing may be conducted by an official of the institution, the official may not be a person who has "a direct interest in the outcome of the hearing." Of course, it can be argued that any officer of the institution is predisposed to uphold the institution's interests against the individual's challenge. But this provision is designed solely to disqualify a person who would be *directly* affected by a decision to amend a record, such as the teacher who placed the disputed information in the record or the administrator who will use the information to make a decision about the student.
4. The student or parent must be given a fair opportunity to present arguments and evidence. He may be accompanied, assisted, or represented by any person or persons of his choice: a family member,

friend, witness, interpreter, lay advocate (such as a student-government representative), or attorney.

5. The hearing decision must be handed down, in writing, within a reasonable time. It must be based solely on evidence presented at the hearing. It must contain a summary of the evidence and the reasons for the decision.

6. If the hearing determines that the information is inaccurate, misleading, or a violation of the privacy or other rights of the student, the record must be amended accordingly, and the student or parent must be so informed in writing.[18]

Although the law is not specific on this point, the burden of proof appears to rest upon the student or parent to persuade the institution that the record should be changed.

What happens if the hearing decision denies the request to amend a record?

The school must inform the eligible student or parent that he has the right to insert into the record a statement setting forth the reasons for his disagreement with the information. That statement must be maintained as a part of the student's records for as long as the disputed information is itself maintained by the institution, and it must be given to anyone to whom the disputed information is disclosed.[19].

If the student or parent believes that the hearing was not conducted in accordance with the standards required by FERPA, he may submit a complaint to the Department of Education (see the explanation for complaint procedures later in this chapter).

May school records be disclosed to outsiders?

Under most circumstances, no, not without the consent of the eligible student or parent.[20]

There are exceptions to the prohibition on disclosure without consent. The most important disclosures permitted without student or parental consent are these:

1. To personnel within the same school or local school district who have "legitimate educational interests" in the information.[21] In practice, this may be interpreted to encompass almost anyone employed by the

school or school district. The educational institution maintaining the records is responsible for defining which people have a "legitimate educational interest."

2. To officials of another school or district in which the student seeks to enroll or is already enrolled. In such cases, copies of the transferred records and the opportunity for a hearing on the accuracy of their contents must be made available to the eligible student or parent, on request.[22]

3. To certain federal and state educational authorities for purposes of enforcing legal requirements in federally supported education programs. These officials must destroy all personally identifiable data they have gathered when their official duties are completed.[23]

4. To persons involved in granting financial aid for which the student has applied, and in enforcing the terms and conditions of aid the student receives.[24]

5. To state and local authorities to whom information is *required* (not merely permitted) to be disclosed under the provisions of a state statute adopted prior to November 19, 1974.[25] These might include state laws requiring reports of suspected child abuse to a state registry, or reports on juvenile offenders to probation and parole officers, or reports of communicable diseases to local and state boards of health.

6. To testing, research, and accrediting organizations, under certain safeguards.[26]

7. Pursuant to a court order or lawfully issued subpoena. The school receiving such an order or subpoena must make a "reasonable effort" to notify the eligible student or parent before it releases the records.[27] Timely notice would give the person the opportunity to contest the validity of the court order or subpoena on his own behalf.

8. In very narrowly defined emergencies affecting the health and safety of the student or other persons.[28]

In addition, there are circumstances, described in greater detail later in this chapter, in which information may be given to students' parents, and in which so-called "directory information" may be released without consent. It should also be remembered that information maintained by campus security officers may be shared with law-enforcement officers in the same jurisdiction, and that certain kinds of medical and psychiatric records may be shared with persons involved in the student's treatment, as stated earlier.[29]

FERPA does not actually require that any of these various categories of records be released without a student's or parent's consent. An educational institution is free to provide consent procedures for these records also. And there are, of course, various state and local laws, regulations, and school-board policies more protective than FERPA, which may ban the release without consent of some kinds of information allowed under FERPA. Where such stronger laws and policies exist, they take precedence over FERPA.[30]

May students withhold their records from their own parents?

Sometimes.

Upon entering college or turning eighteen, the student, known in FERPA as an "eligible student," assumes control of his own FERPA rights, and may prevent any other person—including his parents—from obtaining access to most of his records without his consent.

There is, however, a provision in FERPA allowing a school, in its discretion, to give information to the parents of an eligible student who is a "dependent student" as defined by Section 152 of the Internal Revenue Code of 1954.[31] A dependent student, for tax purposes, is a full-time student whose parents contribute more than half of his support even though he may live away from home and earn some money on his own. The information most frequently given to parents under this provision is the student's grades.

What is "directory information"?

The student's name, address, telephone number, date and place of birth, major field of study, participation in school sports and activities, weight and height of athletic-team members, dates of attendance, degrees and awards, most recent previous school attended, and similar descriptive information.[32]

May directory information be released without consent?

Yes, unless the eligible student or parent directs otherwise.

Each school must compile a list of the categories it intends to classify as directory information. It must give public notice (in the school newspaper, for example) of these categories, inform parents and students of their right to object to the release of information about themselves in any or all of these categories, and allow a sufficient period in which eligible students and parents may exercise that right. The person must inform the school in writing if he objects to the disclosure of particular items about himself or his child. The school is then free to release, without restriction, any directory information to which no objection has been submitted.[33]

It is interesting to note that FERPA extends its most elaborate protections against disclosure without consent to the kinds of personal information least likely to embarrass or prejudice or cause annoyance to a student.[34] On the other hand, students are given no similar opportunity to object to the release of other kinds of records that FERPA permits to be disclosed without consent (described above), and that often contain far more sensitive personal information.

How is consent to disclosure obtained?

Consent must be written. It must be signed and dated by the eligible student or parent. It must specify what records are to be disclosed, the purpose of the disclosure, and the person or class of persons to whom the records are to be disclosed. The eligible student or parent must be given a copy of any record disclosed with his consent, upon request.[35]

How can a student or parent find out what records have been disclosed?

Disclosures must be logged. For each disclosure of a record, and for each request for the disclosure of a record, the school must note who made the request, and what were their "legitimate interests" in requesting or obtaining the record. The disclosure log may be inspected by the parent or eligible student.

A few requests and disclosures need not be logged:

those made to the parent or eligible student himself, those made to personnel within the same school or district who have a "legitimate educational interest" in the record, those made with the consent of the student or parent, and disclosures of directory information.

The disclosure log is considered a part of the student's records, and must be maintained as long as the records themselves are maintained. It is important to note that the log must contain all requests for disclosure, whether or not the requests were actually granted.[36]

Once information from a student's record has been disclosed, is there any way of protecting its confidentiality or preventing its redisclosure to others?

Yes, in theory, though not very effectively in practice.

When the school discloses information with the student's or parent's consent, the recipient must agree to keep it confidential. If the recipient later wants to redisclose the information, it must obtain the student's or parent's consent.

When information is obtained under circumstances not requiring student or parental consent, it may be redisclosed by the recipient only to another person or agency legally entitled to receive it without student or parental consent. The recipient must log any such redisclosure. [37]

FERPA's reassurances against redisclosures are frankly rather shaky. Although the institution releasing the record must inform the recipient that redisclosure is forbidden, no written agreement is required, and the ban has little weight unless the recipient is itself an agency or individual subject to some separate legal obligation to maintain confidentiality. Because of this, students and parents should pay close attention to the log of disclosures maintained in the student's records. It should be checked periodically, to track disclosures and redisclosures of information. If one cannot actually prevent unauthorized redisclosures, it is at least helpful to know what they are.

How is FERPA enforced?

The Department of Education enforces the Family Educational Rights and Privacy Act, through a special FERPA Office in Washington, D.C. This office investigates alleged violations of the act and processes complaints. A review board adjudicates cases not resolved by the FERPA Office.[38]

The Department of Education is also responsible for the regulations that establish standards for the record-keeping procedures of educational institutions subject to FERPA.[39]

Who may file an enforcement complaint, and on what grounds?

Any parent or eligible student may complain to the Department of Education of a violation of any provision of FERPA. Such a violation may concern the student personally: a denial of access to records, a refusal to correct inaccurate information, an unreasonable delay in granting access or correction, a disclosure made without the student's or parent's consent. Or it may concern the record-keeping practices of the institution as they affect the student community as a whole: a failure to establish procedures for access to records, to compile lists of records maintained, to provide for hearings, to publish descriptions of directory information, to log disclosures, to protect records from unauthorized disclosures, to give students and parents annual notice of the fact that they have certain rights under FERPA, or to comply with any other obligation imposed by the statute or regulations.

No infraction is too trivial to be reported to the FERPA Office. But one must bear in mind that the complaint procedure is burdensome and protracted, timely relief is unlikely, and the enforcement mechanism is remote from the ordinary student or parent. Complete reliance upon a formal complaint would be unwise; other avenues of redress, such as general student-grievance procedures, pressure by parent associations and student-government associations, publicity, or even professional legal assistance, may be more productive.

How are complaints processed?

Complaints must be submitted in writing to the FERPA Office, at 200 Independence Avenue, S.W., Washington, D.C. 20201. No special legal form is required, merely a letter setting out the specifics of the alleged violation. It is helpful to append copies of correspondence with the school regarding the dispute.

The FERPA Office will acknowledge its receipt of the

complaint and will inform the school that a complaint has been filed against it, inviting the school to respond. There will follow a period of investigation and negotiation in which the FERPA Office will determine whether a violation has taken place and, if so, exactly what steps the institution must take to rectify its practices within a specified period of time. The complainant will be notified of the office's findings.[40]

In some instances the FERPA Office may be able to determine immediately whether or not a violation has occurred, and the school may comply without delay. But there is no time limit for investigations, and a complicated complaint could drag out for months, particularly if the school is deliberately obstructive. That is why it is advisable to continue other efforts to resolve a dispute even while a formal complaint is pending.

May the courts intervene to adjudicate FERPA complaints?

Probably yes, although FERPA itself does not provide for judicial review, and the courts have not yet stepped into this role. The Privacy Protection Study Commission, in its report of July 1977,[41] recommended that FERPA be amended to permit a parent or eligible student to seek injunctive relief in the courts for any failure by an educational institution to comply with FERPA. Even if the statute is not amended in this way, redress through the courts is an available, if unused, remedy.

What can the Department of Education do if a school does not comply with a decision by the FERPA Office?

Proceedings may be instituted by a special review board to withdraw all federal funds given to the institution through the U.S. Office of Education.[42]

The nature of this ultimate sanction for a violation of FERPA helps explain why students and parents frequently have difficulty exercising their statutory rights with respect to school records. The sanction is wholly disproportionate to the seriousness of most violations, and is therefore most unlikely to be invoked. No one really expects that all federal funding will be withdrawn from a public high school just because it has refused to let a few students examine some of their records. In fact, the withdrawal of funds would harm the students much more than even a major violation of FERPA. Also, the tortuous proceedings required in order to terminate funding completely foreclose any hope of timely relief for the individual whose FERPA rights have been violated. So far, no institution has suffered this final sanction.

What other laws, in addition to FERPA, protect the privacy of students?

A few states have statutes that expand or clarify the rights of access and confidentiality provided by FERPA.[43] The federal statute establishes minimum standards for the maintenance and dissemination of student records, and any further protections available under state legislation take precedence. Such state statutes may apply to certain schools not subject to FERPA, or prohibit the dissemination of some kinds of information from student records that FERPA permits. It should also be remembered, as mentioned earlier, that some state and local school boards, and some educational institutions individually, have adopted policies with respect to school records that expand the rights available under FERPA. These might include the extension of a right of access to students younger than eighteen, or the adoption by a private university, not subject to FERPA, of record-keeping policies similar to those imposed by the federal law.

State freedom-of-information laws and privacy (fair-information-practices) laws contain provisions applicable to the records of students, particularly those personally identifiable records maintained by state and local agencies other than schools. There are many government agencies that collect information about students: public-health departments, child-abuse registries, welfare departments, hospitals, mental-health clinics, police, juvenile courts, parole and probation agencies, social-services agencies, and many more. The laws pertaining to some of these are described in other chapters of this book.

A few states have statutes protecting the confidentiality of communications between students and school counselors.[44] In other states the content of such communications is not legally privileged, although any records maintained by counselors are of course covered by FERPA and applicable state laws.

NOTES

1. 20 U.S.C. 1232g., as amended by Pub. L. No. 96-46 §4(c).
2. 45 C.F.R. 99.1.
3. 20 U.S.C. 1232g(a)(5); 45 C.F.R. 99.3.
4. 20 U.S.C. 1232g(e); 45 C.F.R. 99.5.
5. 20 U.S.C. 1232g(a)(4); 45 C.F.R. 99.3.
6. *Id.*
7. 20 U.S.C. 1232g(a)(1)(B); 45 C.F.R. 99.12.
8. 20 U.S.C. 1232g(a)(1)(B) and (C); 45 C.F.R. 99.7 and 99.12.
9. 20 U.S.C. 1232g(e); 45 C.F.R. 99.6.
10. 20 U.S.C. 1232g(a)(1)(A).
11. 45 C.F.R. 99.11.
12. 45 C.F.R. 99.8.
13. 45 C.F.R. 99.11.
14. 45 C.F.R. 99.8.
15. 45 C.F.R. 99.5.
16. 20 U.S.C. 1232g(a)(2); 45 C.F.R. 99.20.
17. Cong. Rec., S21,488, December 13, 1974.
18. 20 U.S.C. 1232g(a)(2); 45 C.F.R. 99.21 and 99.22.
19. *Id.*
20. 20 U.S.C. 1232g(b).
21. 45 C.F.R. 99.31.
22. 45 C.F.R. 99.31 and 99.34.
23. 45 C.F.R. 99.31 and 99.35.
24. 45 C.F.R. 99.31.
25. *Id.*
26. *Id.*
27. *Id.*
28. 45 C.F.R. 99.31 and 99.36.
29. 45 C.F.R. 99.3.
30. 20 U.S.C. 1232g(b)(1).
31. 45 C.F.R. 99.31.
32. 20 U.S.C. 1232g(a)(5)(A); 45 C.F.R. 99.3.
33. 20 U.S.C. 1232g(a)(5)(A) and (B); 45 C.F.R. 99.37.
34. Privacy Protection Study Commission, Personal Privacy in an Information Society 427 (U.S. Government Printing Office, July 1977).
35. 20 U.S.C. 1232g(b)(1) and (b)(2)(A); 45 C.F.R. 99.30.
36. 20 U.S.C. 1232g(b)(4)(A); 45 C.F.R. 99.32.
37. 20 U.S.C. 1232g(b)(4)(B).
38. 20 U.S.C. 1232g(g).
39. 45 C.F.R. 99.
40. 45 C.F.R. 99.63.
41. Privacy Protection Study Commission, *supra* note 34, at

438. See, however, Girardier v. Webster College, 563 F.2d 1267 (8th Cir.; 1977).

42. 20 U.S.C. 1232g(f); 45 C.F.R. 99.64–67.

43. *See, e.g.,* CAL. EDUC. CODE §§967, 10931, 22509, and 25430; CONN. GEN. STAT. ANN. §10–156; DEL. CODE ANN. tit. 41, §4114; ILL. REV. STAT. ch. 122, §§50–1 *et seq.;* MASS. ANN. LAWS ch. 71, §340; MISS. CODE ANN. §37–15–1; NEB. REV. STAT. §§79–4, 156 and 157; WIS. STAT. ANN. §118.125.

44. *See* CONN. GEN. STAT. ANN. §10–154; IDAHO CODE §9–203; KY. REV. STAT. §421.216; ME. REV. STAT. ANN. tit. 20, §806; MONT. REV. CODES ANN. §§93–701 *et seq.;* NEV. REV. STAT. §§49.290 *et seq.;* N.C. GEN. STAT. §8–53.4; N.D. CENT. CODE §31–01–06.1; S.D. COMPILED LAWS ANN. §§19–2–5.1 and 5.2.

III

Financial Records

Should people assume that their bank records are confidential?

No.

Despite a common impression to the contrary, the records maintained by banks describing the financial affairs of a customer—deposits, withdrawals, checks, interest payments, loans, overdrafts, and so on—do not "belong" to the customer. According to a 1976 U.S. Supreme Court ruling, these records are merely the records of commercial transactions, not confidential communications, and they "belong" to the bank, not to the customer. For these reasons, said the Court, a bank customer has no constitutionally "legitimate expectation of privacy" in his bank records, and no legal "standing" to prevent the bank from revealing the records to others.[1]

Bank records are therefore confidential only to the extent that federal and state statutes forbid certain government officials or private parties from obtaining access to them without the customer's consent. These statutes are limited in their scope, and where they do not reach, the confidentiality of a person's bank records is at the mercy of the bank's discretion. Furthermore, that discretion is shaped by legal record-keeping and reporting requirements, notably under the Bank Secrecy Act, that facilitate access by government officials to the records of individual bank customers.

How does the Bank Secrecy Act affect the confidentiality of bank records?

The Bank Secrecy Act of 1970 [2] places legal obligations upon banks to maintain certain records of their customers' transactions for specific periods, and to report certain of those transactions to the federal government.

The law mandates the U.S. Treasury Department to write detailed regulations interpreting the requirements of the act.[3]

The act's original purpose was to force U.S. citizens to disclose their foreign accounts and foreign currency transactions in order to prevent circumvention of U.S. currency and tax laws. It is required, for example, that banks maintain records of instructions from their customers concerning the transmission of funds, currency, and credit out of the country in amounts over $10,000, and that travelers report the transportation into or out of the U.S. of currency in amounts over $5000.

Of greater concern to the ordinary bank customer are the provisions that banks must keep, for five years, a microfilmed copy of the front and back of every check over $100, all account statements, all signature-authority documents, and all records necessary to reconstruct a checking account and furnish an audit trial for transactions over $100. The act and regulations require brokers and banks to obtain the customer's Social Security number or other taxpayer identification number for trading and deposit accounts, and require banks to report to the Internal Revenue Service any "unusual" domestic currency transaction of more than $2500.

The practical result of these and other provisions of the act and its regulations is that every record of every transaction by every customer is preserved and potentially available for government examination. (The $100 cut-off figure for the check-recording requirement is meaningless, because the banks find it much too expensive to sort out checks for amounts under $100. Therefore, microfilms are taken of all checks, front and back, and kept for five years.)

If, as the highest California state court once observed, a person's bank records are the mirror of his life, "a virtual current biography," [4] the implementation of the Bank Secrecy Act produces a complete, permanent image of the customer's personal, private life. And because, according to the U.S. Supreme Court, a person has no constitutional expectation of privacy in his bank records, that image is potentially accessible to government officials without the person's consent, in some cases even without his knowledge.

Despite the scope of the act and of the Treasury Department regulations, and despite their clear implications for the right of financial privacy, in 1974 the U.S. Supreme Court upheld the constitutionality of the act against a challenge based on the First Amendment right of privacy of association, the Fourth Amendment right to freedom from unreasonable search and seizure, and the Fifth Amendment privilege against self-incrimination.[5] Although Congress subsequently enacted the Right to Financial Privacy Act of 1978 to provide some statutory protections for bank records, this Supreme Court decision on the Bank Secrecy Act and the Court's 1976 ruling mentioned earlier place the bank customer in a very vulnerable position with respect to any reasonable expectation that his bank records will be protected from access by government officials.

Why do government agencies seek access to bank records?

Bank records are often used by the police, prosecutors, and other law-enforcement officials in criminal investigations. Until the enactment of the federal Right to Financial Privacy Act of 1978, FBI agents were able to obtain a customer's bank records merely by presenting themselves to a bank's security chief and announcing that an investigation in progress required the records of a certain customer, or even a search through the records of many customers. Such informal examination of bank records was a common occurrence in the police and FBI surveillance of antiwar and civil-rights organizations and "radical" political parties of both right and left in the 1950s, 1960s, and early 1970s. Except in a few states that have enacted their own bank-privacy laws, local and state law-enforcement officials are still free to rummage around in a bank customer's records in this manner.

Local, state, and federal tax authorities and other agencies charged with the enforcement of tax, securities, and financial laws naturally find personal bank records very useful, either in their routine administrative procedures or in criminal investigations. The Bank Secrecy Act record-keeping requirements are intended to increase the amount of personal bank information available to these agencies, because such records "have a high degree of usefulness in criminal, tax, and regulatory investigations and proceedings." [6]

Determinations of an individual's eligibility for a government benefit or participation in a government program often involve an examination of his bank records. Usually, this is done with the formality of the individual's written consent, although he really has very little choice in the matter and often is obliged to authorize access to all of his bank records rather than to specific information.

How does the federal Right to Financial Privacy Act protect bank customers against government access to their records?

The Right to Financial Privacy Act forbids an official or employee of a federal agency to obtain or examine the bank records of any person without that person's consent, except pursuant to formal legal process—an administrative subpoena or summons, a search warrant, a judicial subpoena (court order), or a formal written request.[7] (The provision for a "formal written request" is limited to agencies that do not have the authority to issue administrative subpoenas or summonses.)

It is important to bear in mind that the act restricts the actions only of *federal*, not state or local, officials. Therefore, its strictures apply to agents of the FBI, investigators of the Justice and Treasury Departments, and employees of the Social Security Administration, for example, but not to local or state tax-agency investigators, welfare administrators, or police.

There are important exceptions to the prohibitions on access to a bank customer's records by federal agents, among them the following: [8]

1. "Emergency access" is permitted without any formal process if a federal-agency official of supervisory rank determines that immediate access is necessary because of the imminent danger of physical injury to any person, serious property damage, or flight to avoid prosecution. If emergency access is obtained, the agency must file a sworn explanatory statement with a federal district court within five days, and must thereafter notify the bank customer that his records have been obtained.

2. Foreign-intelligence and counterintelligence agents and Secret Service agents performing protective functions (guarding the President) are permitted to obtain bank records merely by request. In such instances, the bank releasing the customer's records to the federal agent is forbidden to disclose to *anyone* the fact that the records were sought or obtained.

3. Such supervisory and regulatory agencies as the Federal Deposit Insurance Corporation, the Federal Reserve Board, the Securities and Exchange Commission, and analogous state banking and securities agencies are permitted to examine bank records in accordance with existing statutes that define their functions. The Secretary of the Treasury is permitted to examine bank records in accordance with the Bank Secrecy Act, its interpretive regulations, and the Foreign Transactions Reporting Act. Access by Internal Revenue Service agents is governed by the Internal Revenue Code.

4. When the customer is under consideration for a federal loan, loan guarantee, or loan insurance program, the appropriate agency may examine his bank records without formal legal process.

5. Normal procedures for obtaining records under the U.S. Code and Federal Rules of Civil and Criminal Procedure apply when the records are sought in the course of litigation to which the government is a party.

6. When disclosures of bank records to federal agencies are required by any other federal law or regulation, the Right to Financial Privacy Act does not override such requirements.

In addition to the restrictions placed upon the powers of federal agencies to obtain records, the act places certain obligations upon banks to protect the rights of their customers. A bank is not permitted to release a customer's records to a federal agency except in accordance with the requirements of the statute. However, the bank is permitted to notify a federal agency of the fact that it has in its possession information that may be relevant to a possible violation of a law or regulation.[9] Then, to obtain that information, the agency would have to comply with the applicable procedures required by the statute.

How does a bank customer authorize disclosures of his records under the Right to Financial Privacy Act?

An authorization must be written, signed, dated, and presented to both the bank and the federal agency that will receive the records. No authorization is valid for more than three months, and it may be revoked at any time during those three months. The authorization must specify which records are to be disclosed and the purposes for which the government will use them, and must notify the customer of his rights under the act.

No financial institution may require a customer's authorization as a condition of doing business.[10]

How are federal government agencies limited in the purposes for which they may seek a person's bank records by a subpoena, summons, warrant, or formal written request?

These methods are to be used when agencies are seeking access to bank records for law-enforcement purposes—other than those specific law-enforcement purposes for which the act permits access without any formal legal process (see listing above).

To obtain bank records pursuant to an administrative subpoena or summons, a court order, or a formal written request, the agency need only have "reason to believe that the records sought are relevant to a legitimate law enforcement inquiry." To obtain bank records pursuant to a search warrant, the agency must meet a higher standard of "probable cause" to believe that an offense has been or is about to be committed and that the bank records will yield pertinent evidence.[11] The higher standard required for a search warrant is complemented by the agency's freedom to obtain the records without delay or prior notification to the bank customer.

How does the customer know that his bank records are being sought or have been obtained by a federal agency?

If the agency seeks access to the records by an administrative subpoena or summons, a court order, or a formal written request, the agency must serve or mail a copy to the customer at his last known address; this must be done on or before the date when it is served upon the bank. At the same time, the agency must give the customer a written explanation of (1) the nature of the law-enforcement inquiry to which the records are believed "relevant," and (2) the Right to Financial Privacy Act's provisions whereby a customer may challenge the agency's attempt to obtain the records. The agency may not actually obtain the records from the bank until ten days after notice has been served to the customer or fourteen days after it has been mailed.

If the agency seeks access with a search warrant, it may notify the customer at any time within ninety days after the warrant is served upon the bank. Once a warrant has been served, the bank must release the records immediately.

However, the act also allows agencies to delay notice to the customer, for successive periods of ninety days, by the authorization of a federal district court. The agency must satisfy the court that its law-enforcement investigation is within the agency's lawful jurisdiction, that the records are relevant, and that immediate notice to the customer might result in one of the following:

1. danger to the life or physical safety of any person;
2. flight from prosecution;
3. destruction of or tampering with evidence;
4. intimidation of potential witnesses; or
5. serious jeopardy to the investigation or undue delay of a trial or official proceeding.

These generous conditions could in practice easily be applied to justify an indefinite delay of notification to a bank customer simply because an agency does not wish to be bothered by a customer's challenge to its request for access.

After the delay granted by the court expires, the agency must serve or mail to the customer a notice stating that specified records have been obtained for use in an investigation whose purpose is described.

If an agency obtains access to records under the act's emergency provisions described earlier, it must notify the customer "as soon as practicable" thereafter. However, if the records are obtained by foreign-intelligence or Secret Service agents, the customer will never be informed.[12]

If records are sought with a customer's own authorization, the bank must keep an accounting of all disclosures it makes under the authorization and make that accounting available to the customer on request—unless an agency obtains a court order permitting delay of such notification.[18]

In summary: in circumstances for which the Right to Financial Privacy Act requires a federal agency to follow some form of legal process in order to obtain a customer's records, the customer will normally receive notice of the agency's request for the records before the records are actually released by the bank. However, there are many circumstances in which agencies may obtain records without legal process, and therefore often without the customer's knowledge, and also many circumstances in which an agency can avoid its obligations to notify the customer by making certain representations to a court.

As a practical matter, therefore, it is a mistake to believe that one's bank records have not been disclosed to a federal agency simply because one has not received a notification under the Right to Financial Privacy Act.

Another method of learning whether a federal agency may have obtained information from one's bank records is to use the access provisions of the Freedom of Information Act to examine the records maintained by a federal agency, as outlined in Chapter XIV. Although certain federal-agency investigative records cannot be obtained under the FOIA, sufficient information might be accessible to suggest that the agency had, in fact, examined bank records.

Assuming that the customer does receive prior notice, what can he do?

He may challenge in court the agency's attempt to obtain his bank records. To do so, he must state to the court his reasons for believing that the records are not relevant to the law-enforcement inquiry cited by the government (thus, perhaps, being forced to reveal some of the very information he is trying to protect), or that the government has not substantially complied with the requirements of the act. The court must then decide whether the government's investigation is a legitimate one, whether the records sought are in fact relevant, and whether the agency has substantially complied with all required procedures. On this basis, the court will either grant or deny the agency's request. In a highly controversial provision—certain to be tested eventually in the courts—the act limits the customer's challenge to these stated procedures, thus appearing to prevent any attempt to mount a challenge on other statutory grounds, or even on constitutional grounds.[14]

The agency's notification to the customer will state that it is not necessary to have an attorney in order to challenge the agency's action in court. But it is not wise to attempt such a potentially complex procedure without expert legal advice; anyone who receives notice that his bank records are being sought and who wishes to resist should consult an attorney if possible.

Once a federal agency has obtained a customer's records, may it pass them on to other agencies?

Yes, if the agency certifies in writing that the transfer is being made because it believes that the records are relevant to a legitimate law-enforcement inquiry within the jurisdiction of the receiving agency. Notice of such a transfer must be given to the customer within fourteen days, until the agency obtains a court order permitting delay of notification.[15]

Are there any laws protecting bank customers against the disclosure of their records to state authorities?

Yes. A few states have enacted bank-privacy statutes that require a state or local government agency to obtain bank records only by formal legal process.[16] A number of these are more stringent in their restrictions upon state agencies than the federal statute is with respect to federal agencies.

However, in the vast majority of states, where no such statutes have been adopted, state and local police and other authorities can still legally obtain a customer's bank records merely by an informal, unwritten request to the bank. It is then left entirely to the discretion of the bank whether to comply.

Bank policies on these matters vary widely. Some banks will respond only to formal legal process, others to a written request on the agency's official stationery. Some allow their branches a certain degree of discretion, so that particular branch managers or security chiefs may even comply with oral requests from government officials.

Banks also vary on the question of prior notification to the customer. Some adhere to strict policies in this regard and take upon themselves the responsibility for informing the customer that his records have been subpoenaed. In other banks the matter is handled on a case-by-case basis by their own legal counsel, who may be persuaded in particular circumstances to honor an agency's request that a customer not be notified.

What this means to the individual bank customer is simply that the privacy of his records is at the mercy of his banker. That being so, it is a good idea to ask one's bank for a written statement of its policies with regard to government demands for customer records.

May banks release information from a customer's records to a third party that is not a government agency?

Yes. Ordinary business practice governs many situations in which a private party having some business or financial relationship with a customer (such as a creditor) may obtain information about him from his bank. Often, the customer is informed that this will be necessary and is asked to give his consent. But not invariably: banks will reveal information about a customer to independent check-guarantee or check-verification services, to collection agencies, to credit-reporting agencies and credit bureaus, or to individual credit grantors without the customer's consent. Banks follow their own individual policies as to how much and what kinds of information they will reveal in each of these circumstances, and as to any notice, before or after the fact, to the customer. (For restrictions upon credit-reporting agencies that handle information obtained from banks, see Chapter IV.)

There is a growing common-law doctrine of the duty of confidentiality that banks owe their customers, developed through a series of state court decisions,[17] which suggests that banks have a legal obligation not to disclose information about their customers to private third parties. The thrust of these decisions is that customers may be able to protect themselves from certain exceptional disclosures to private third parties, especially when the disclosures might cause some tangible (usually financial) harm to the customer. However, they would not apply to disclosures made in the course of ordinary business practice—which many people find no less offensive for being ordinary—and they do not overcome the presumptions, enunciated in the Supreme Court decisions mentioned earlier, that the records are the "property" of the bank and are merely the notations of commercial transactions, not confidential communications.

What laws protect the confidentiality of federal tax records?

Under the Tax Reform Act of 1976, amending the Internal Revenue Code,[18] federal tax returns and other personal information submitted to or collected by the Internal Revenue Service may not be revealed to anyone outside the IRS without the individual's authorization, except for specifically enumerated purposes.

The major exceptions to the confidentiality provisions of the Tax Reform Act, permitting disclosure of a taxpayer's return or return information without his authorization, are as follows:

1. To state tax officials, upon the written request of the head of a state tax agency or commission.
2. To persons having a "material interest." Such persons might include trustees, spouses, business partners, guardians of a legally incompetent taxpayer, or receivers of the property of a bankrupt taxpayer.
3. To certain committees of the Congress. If a particular taxpayer is or could be identified in the returns disclosed, the Congressional committee may receive them only while sitting in closed session, unless the taxpayer consents in writing to the disclosure in an open session.
4. To the President and certain White House officials designated by the President. This may be done only upon the President's written request, specifying the information sought and the reasons for the request. All such requests must be reported to the Joint Congressional Committee on Taxation. The act contains special provisions allowing presidential scrutiny of tax information concerning candidates for appoint-

ment to certain federal executive or judicial positions.

5. To employees of the Treasury Department and the Department of Justice for purposes of enforcing the tax laws. For example, returns or return information may be released to a U.S. Attorney in contemplation of a proceeding before a federal grand jury or federal or state court concerning a violation of the tax laws. Under some circumstances, a taxpayer's return could be disclosed pursuant to this provision even if that particular taxpayer is not himself the target of the investigation or prosecution.

6. To attorneys for use in screening prospective jurors in a tax case. This highly controversial provision, which was opposed by the Privacy Protection Study Commission,[19] permits both the government's attorneys and the attorneys for the defense to ask the IRS whether a prospective juror has ever been the subject of an IRS audit or investigation. The purported reason for such disclosures is to weed out jurors who may harbor personal resentments against the IRS, but the Privacy Commission called the value of such information "marginal" and pointed out that the same information can be obtained by direct questioning of the prospective juror in court.

7. To another federal agency for purposes of administering federal laws other than the tax laws. In a non-tax criminal investigation, a taxpayer's return or return information may be disclosed by the order of a federal district court judge. The judge must determine that there is reasonable cause to believe that a specific criminal act has been committed, that the return contains evidence related to the crime, and that the same evidence could not reasonably be obtained from some other source. The taxpayer need not be informed of the judicial proceeding by which the release of his tax records is authorized, and so has no opportunity to contest the disclosure. Additionally, the IRS may disclose to other federal agencies for use in non-tax criminal investigations certain information in its possession that comes from a source other than the taxpayer's own return, and may make disclosures of this kind without any court order. Such other sources might be bank or credit-

card records previously obtained by the IRS, or an informant.

8. To certain other agencies for specified purposes, such as the administration of the Social Security and Railroad Retirement Acts, the location of missing parents under child-support enforcement programs, and the notification through the press of persons to whom IRS owes refunds.

Federal and state officials (including former officials) who make disclosures of taxpayer information not authorized by this statute can be punished by imprisonment up to five years and a fine up to $5000. In addition, the aggrieved taxpayer may bring a civil action to recover actual damages against officials who knowingly or negligently make an unauthorized disclosure, and for punitive damages in addition if the official acted willfully or with gross negligence.[20]

What about state tax records?

Most states have statutes protecting the confidentiality of information submitted to or gathered by state tax authorities. These vary widely in the safeguards they provide and in the disclosures they permit.

The Tax Reform Act of 1976 requires state tax authorities to establish administrative safeguards for the confidentiality of information they receive from the IRS. If a state requires a taxpayer to submit a copy of his federal tax return along with his state return, the act provides that the state must have statutory, not merely administrative, safeguards for the confidentiality of tax information.[21] In general, protections against the unauthorized disclosure of either federal or state tax information by state authorities are weaker and harder to enforce than those applicable to the IRS itself.

May a person have access to his own tax records?

Yes. Rights of access to and correction of one's own tax records (including not only returns but also information collected by the tax agency from other sources) are governed by the federal Privacy Act, in the case of IRS records, and by analogous state privacy statutes where these have been enacted. These statutes can also be used to determine what disclosures of personal information have been made by tax agencies to other agencies or persons. In states that do not have privacy acts, a state freedom-of-information law can often be used to obtain access to one's own state tax records.

If a person believes that his bank or tax records have been disclosed illegally, what should he do?

Consult a lawyer. The statutes and regulations concerning financial privacy are extremely complex and vary widely from state to state. Expert legal advice is necessary to determine whether a violation of law has occurred and what remedies might be available.

NOTES

1. U.S. v. Miller, 425 U.S. 435 (1976).
2. 31 U.S.C. 1051 *et seq.*
3. These are published at 31 C.F.R. 103.
4. Burrows v. Superior Court, 13 Cal. 3d 238 (1974).
5. California Bankers Association v. Schultz, 416 U.S. 21 (1974).
6. 31 U.S.C. 1051.
7. 12 U.S.C. 3401 *et seq.*
8. *Id.* §§3413, 3414.
9. *Id.* §3403.
10. *Id.* §3404.
11. *Id.* §3404.
12. *Id.* §§3405–8.
13. *Id.* 3409 and 3414(a)(3).
14. *Id.* §3410.
15. *Id.* §3412.
16. *See* OR. REV. STAT. §§192.550–595; MD. ANN. CODE art. 11, §§224 *et seq.;* ALASKA STAT. §06.05.175; ILL. REV. STAT. ch. 16½, §48.1; CAL. GOV'T. CODE, §§7460 *et seq.*
17. *See* Privacy Protection Study Commission, Personal Privacy in an Information Society (U.S. Government Printing Office, July 1977), Appendix I, Privacy Law in the States 25–27.
18. Pub. L. No. 94–455, §1202, amending 26 U.S.C. 6103.
19. Privacy Protection Study Commission, Personal Privacy in an Information Society, 545.
20. 26 U.S.C. 7217.
21. 26 U.S.C. 6103(p).

IV

Credit Records and Consumer Reports

What is a "credit record"?

The term "credit record," in its narrow sense, refers to information describing a person's previous financial transactions which bear on his present creditworthiness. But in its more general and commonly used sense, the term refers to any information describing a person's financial and employment history, state of health, character, reputation, and style of living that may be used in deciding whether to give that person a loan, credit, an insurance policy, a job, a professional or business license, or some other commercial benefit.

Credit records are compiled primarily by credit bureaus, investigative-reporting agencies, and private-detective agencies, which sell their services to "subscribers"—creditors, employers, and insurers who need to make background checks on prospective borrowers, employees, and policyholders. Merchants' protective associations, cooperative loan exchanges, and other nonprofit groups may also perform credit-reporting services, without charge or at a nominal fee, for their members. All these agencies and organizations maintain permanent, often computerized records on the subjects of their investigations, and many are affiliated in local, regional, or national associations that exchange credit records among their members.

The giant of reporting agencies is Equifax, Inc., formerly known as Retail Credit Company, with headquarters in Atlanta, Georgia. At any one time, Equifax has files on some 39 million individuals nationwide.[1] Of two thousand credit bureaus, the five largest maintain a total of 150 million credit records.[2] The industry as a whole is estimated to gross over $1 billion a year in revenues, and to keep files on over 200 million people. Anyone who has ever applied for a job, an insurance policy, or a loan or credit is likely to be the subject of one of those files.

The investigation conducted by a reporting agency may be limited to the formal records of a person's financial resources and history: sources of income, payment of bills, bad debts, bankruptcies, suits, garnishments, tax liens, etc. A simple credit report of this kind is most often required for a loan or a credit card. But the inquiry may go beyond this, to include interviews with neighbors, employers, landlords, family, and friends for information about the person's life style, character, and general reputation within the community, as well as contacts with the police, doctors, hospitals, insurance companies, and schools. These more wide-ranging searches are called investigative reports, and are frequently conducted for prospective employers and insurers.

Both simple credit reports and the broader investigative reports—together known under the general term "consumer reports"—are regulated by a federal statute called the Fair Credit Reporting Act of 1970 (FCRA).[3] In addition, about a dozen states have credit-reporting statutes similar to the federal law. A few states have enacted laws that place more stringent restrictions on the operations of consumer-reporting agencies; these will be described later in this chapter.

Which records are regulated by the Fair Credit Reporting Act?

The FCRA applies only to records containing information about an individual (not a business) and intended for use in decisions concerning the granting of:

1. personal credit;
2. personal, family, or household insurance;
3. employment;
4. a license or other government benefit for which consideration of a person's financial responsibility or status is required by law;
5. any other "legitimate business need" involving a business transaction with the individual—for example, the renting of an apartment to a tenant.

The act applies only to information collected and transmitted *by a third party*.[4] Thus, a reference given directly by a former employer to a prospective employer, describing his own personal experience with an individual, is not a consumer report within the meaning of the statute. Nor is a direct communication from department store A to department store B, describing how prompt or delinquent a particular customer has been in paying bills at department store A. But if an outside agency transmits that information from a former to a prospective employer, or from store A to store B, it becomes a consumer report under the FCRA.

Both the courts and the Federal Trade Commission (FTC, which has responsibility for the administrative enforcement of the statute) have attempted to clarify specific kinds of reports to which the FCRA applies, often with confusing or contradictory results. For example, under a formal interpretation issued by the FTC, the U.S. Civil Service, although it collects and disseminates information on current and prospective employees of the federal government in much the same way that a credit-reporting agency might handle such information, has been determined not to fall within the scope of FCRA.[5] While a U.S. district court in California ruled the FCRA applicable to a report compiled in connection with the payment of an insurance claim,[6] the FTC interpreted the act as inapplicable to such reports, except when they are later used in a decision to cancel, refuse to renew, or increase the premiums for an insurance policy.[7] The act has been held by a state court in Washington to cover a report originally compiled for a personal health-insurance policy when it was later used again for a business insurance policy.[8] In a much-disputed interpretation by a U.S. district court in Georgia, it was held not to cover the report of a polygraph test transmitted by a polygraph examiner to a prospective employer.[9]

Because these and other cases involving the FCRA's coverage are unclear, and because the legislative history suggests that Congress intended a broad rather than a restrictive interpretation, for practical purposes it is best to assume that if a report was compiled or used for any of the five general purposes enumerated above, it falls within the scope of the act.

Is there any restriction on the kinds of information that may be contained in a credit record?

The federal statute forbids only certain "obsolete information." It is the absence of any effective restriction on the contents of credit records that accounts for the most serious abuses of privacy in consumer reporting.

The FCRA requires in general that agencies implement "reasonable procedures" (undefined) to assure the accuracy of information,[10] but has nothing to say about the propriety or relevance of information. Many reports contain items about people's sex lives, drinking habits, housekeeping standards, politics, social relationships, and marital problems. Even if such items are no more than unsubstantiated tidbits of malicious neighborhood gossip, the FCRA does not prevent their dissemination to would-be employers or creditors. In fact, information about the most private areas of a person's life is routine in most investigative reports. (Simple credit reports tend to concentrate on the objective records of one's financial dealings, although there are exceptions.)

The FCRA does place time limits on the reporting of certain kinds of "adverse information." [11] Adverse information obtained from field investigations and interviews is not supposed to be included in a report if it has not been received or verified within the last three months. Bankruptcies more than fourteen years old may not be reported. Suits, tax liens, and accounts placed for collection may not be reported after seven years. Arrests, indictments, and convictions may not be reported more than seven years after disposition, release, or parole. Seven years is also the limit on all "other adverse information." But even these restrictions do not apply if a report is to be used in connection with credit or insurance of $50,000 or more, or employment at a salary of $20,000 or more.

Under some state fair-credit-reporting acts, notably those in New York and Maine,[12] time limits are placed on other items, and certain kinds of information are barred altogether. New York, for example, does not permit a consumer-reporting agency to report an arrest or criminal charge not followed by a conviction, unless charges are still pending. Nor may it handle information relating to a person's race, religion, color, ancestry, or ethnic origin, or any information "which it has reason to know is inaccurate." For most purposes, information relating to drug or alcohol addiction or confinement in a mental institution may not be reported after seven years. In addition to these restrictions, Maine requires that all information be "reasonably relevant to the purpose for which it is sought" and bans reports dealing with a person's political affiliation or characterizing his personal life style. A few other states forbid the reporting of arrests and indictments not followed by conviction.[13]

It is important to understand that these restrictions apply only to reports made by consumer-reporting agencies. Except where other laws or regulations forbid it, an insurer, creditor, employer, or licensing body might be able to obtain such information from another source.

Can a consumer-reporting agency get information from records that are legally confidential?

Yes.

Applicants for employment, insurance, credit, licenses, and other benefits are frequently asked to sign a waiver of confidentiality or authorization of access that is so broadly worded that it applies to virtually all personal records. Armed with such a waiver, the reporting agency may be able to obtain access to all kinds of confidential records, including hospital, police, and school records. Most people do not realize the significance of what they are signing, and those who do may be afraid to refuse for fear of losing the job or benefits they are trying to obtain. Although some custodians of these confidential records may refuse to honor a general waiver and insist upon a specific authorization for the release of designated records, few can be counted upon to do so.

It is difficult to resist a demand that one sign a general waiver of confidentiality. In some circumstances it may be possible to ask for an enumeration of the specific records that will be sought and to reword the authorization accordingly. It may also be feasible to place a termination date upon the authorization—say thirty or sixty days hence —so that it cannot be filed away and reused.

Another method by which consumer-reporting agencies get legally confidential information is by obtaining it from a source other than the confidential record. The most common example of this practice is the arrest record. In many jurisdictions, law-enforcement agencies are prohibited by law or regulation from giving out information on a particular person's past arrests. But the police blotter—the day-to-day compilation of arrests maintained at the precinct house or police headquarters—is a public record, and in many communities it is published in its entirety in the daily paper. Local consumer-reporting agencies often clip these listings and index them for use in future reports. When local agencies are linked into regional or national associations, such records can be disseminated far beyond the community where the arrest took place. Of course, the blotter does not contain information on the disposition of the arrest, such as a later dismissal of charges or acquittal, and so neither does the report that goes to the employer or insurer.

Finally, there have been a few instances in which consumer-reporting agencies obtained confidential records by deception or fraud. For example, the investigator may represent himself as a doctor in a telephone call to the medical-records department of a hospital, or even show up dressed in a white coat. Occasionally, an investigator may have a friend in the police department or hospital-records room who simply hands over any information he asks for. Many of these practices are legally prohibited (though still difficult to prevent); [14] others have not yet been addressed by legislation.

How does a person know if he is the subject of a consumer report, or if a report will be compiled?

The only sure way to find out if such a report exists would be to write to every investigative-reporting agency, credit bureau, loan exchange, merchants' association, and private detective agency—obviously an impossibility. Because the FCRA does not require a consumer-reporting agency to notify every individual on whom it opens a file, most people remain unaware of the existence of such reports until after they have been turned down for a loan, job, or insurance policy and have been told that it was because of "adverse information" in a consumer report.

The FCRA does not require a report user (that is, the employer, creditor, or insurer who will use the information to make a decision about an individual) to tell an applicant that a simple credit report has been or will be compiled. Only when the user wants a full investigative report—one involving interviews with third parties to determine reputation, living style, and so forth—must he provide prior written notification to the subject. (An exception to the notification requirement is for an investigative report to be used for employment in a position for which the person has not specifically applied. Thus, a person's life can be subjected to covert scrutiny merely because an employer may have an interest in him, even though he has expressed no interest in the employer. This is the "headhunter" exception, created for executive-search agencies.)

The required notification is usually placed somewhere on the insurance, credit, or employment application, and is often couched in very general language. The applicant has the right to request and receive a more "complete and accurate" written description of the "nature and scope" of the investigation, but still won't know which reporting agency will be making the report.[15] (The applicant may attempt, at this point, to obtain an enumeration of specific records that will be sought and persons who will be contacted as a part of the investigation, as was discussed above in connection with general waivers of confidentiality. The statute does not say exactly what constitutes a "complete and accurate" description.)

If the employment, insurance, credit, or other benefit is refused, or if the credit or insurance is offered at an increased charge, and if this decision is based partly or wholly upon information in a consumer report, the report user must reveal to the subject the name and address of the reporting agency.[16] As a practical matter, then, a person will ordinarily learn about his credit record only after the information in it has been used to make an adverse decision about him.

What if an adverse decision is based on information not obtained from a consumer-reporting agency?

If credit for personal, family, or household purposes is denied, or the charges for such credit increased, and if that action is based wholly or in part on information obtained from a source other than a consumer-reporting agency, the FCRA requires that the creditor disclose the reasons for the decision if the credit applicant submits a written request within sixty days after learning of the decision. The creditor must inform the applicant of his right to submit such a request when the adverse decision is made known to him.[17]

This provision for notification does not apply to adverse decisions involving employment or insurance.

Does the government have access to consumer reports?
Yes. A government agency may obtain a consumer report like any other employer, insurer, or creditor. It may also obtain a report if it is required by law to consider a person's financial responsibility or status before granting a license or other benefit. When a government agency obtains a report for these purposes, it is bound by the rules and restrictions the FCRA places upon all users of consumer reports.

But the FCRA also permits consumer-reporting agencies to give some information to a government agency for other purposes. Upon the government's request, it may reveal the following: a person's name, address, former addresses, and present and former places of employment.[18] Thus, if a government agency is looking for a fugitive from justice, it can obtain this "identifying information" from a consumer-reporting agency's files.

The statute leaves to the consumer-reporting agency the responsibility for determining whether a government agency's request is for a "permissible purpose" (thus qualifying for a full consumer report) or for some other purpose (thus limited to identifying information). That determination will rest heavily upon what the government chooses to tell the reporting agency. In practice, it is unlikely that a consumer-reporting agency will very strongly resist a government demand for more than mere identifying information. It must also be remembered that even if a government agency is stymied in its attempt to get certain information from a consumer-reporting agency, it may be successful in obtaining the same information directly from an employer, credit-card company, bank, insurance company, hospital, or other such record custodian.

Aside from the special provisions applying to government agencies, can anyone at all obtain information from a consumer-reporting agency?

No.

Agencies are permitted to prepare and disseminate reports only for the "permissible purposes" enumerated in the FCRA: for use in decisions concerning the granting of credit, insurance, employment, license or other government benefit, or other "legitimate business need" in connection with a business transaction involving the subject of the report. The agency must take reasonable measures to verify the identity of report users and to assure that a report will be used only for a permissible purpose.[19] The FCRA provides for criminal penalties—up to $5000 or a year in prison or both—for anyone who obtains information from a consumer-reporting agency "under false pretenses" [20] (for example, someone who poses as a prospective employer), or for an employee of a consumer-reporting agency who "knowingly and willfully" provides information to an unauthorized recipient.[21]

May people learn the contents of their own credit records?

Yes, up to a point. The FCRA says that a person, upon request to the consumer-reporting agency, must be told "the nature and substance" of the information in his record.[22] This means the person need not be allowed to read the record for himself, or have it read to him word for word, or obtain a copy of it. Under some state statutes, however, a person may either read or obtain a copy of his records, or both.[23]

Two kinds of information in a credit record need not be revealed to the subject under the FCRA. One is medical information obtained from physicians, hospitals, and other medical personnel and facilities.[24] The other is the identity of the sources of information collected solely for use in an investigative report.[25] (Sources of information used in a simple credit report *are* subject to disclosure.) For example, if in an interview for an investigative report a neighbor said that the subject is a drug user or has a reputation for cheating on his wife, the neighbor's identity as the source of that information would not be revealed, except by court order in a lawsuit.

The agency must reveal to the subject the names of any recipient of a report on him within the last two years for employment purposes, or within the last six months for any other purpose.[26]

How can people examine their credit records?

A consumer-reporting agency must respond to a person's request for access to his own records during normal business hours and upon "reasonable notice." The individual may appear in person, or may request disclosure by telephone. He must furnish personal identification, and may be accompanied by one other person of his own choosing. Telephone and travel costs are borne by the individual.[27]

The agency is obliged, under the FCRA, to provide trained personnel to explain the contents of the record.[28] However, many people report that they have encountered agency employees who are poorly prepared, even openly hostile and obstructive, and in the absense of a statutory right of physical access to one's own record or to a copy of its contents (available only in a few states), there is no sure way of judging whether the agency's oral summary is either accurate or complete.

The agency may charge a "reasonable fee" for disclosing the contents of a record to the subject. The fee must be specified before the interview. An exception is made for people who request access to their records within thirty days of an adverse decision (such as denial of employment or an increase in insurance rates) resulting from information in a consumer report. In such cases, no charge may be levied.[29]

In spite of the difficulties, frustrations, and expenses, it is important to examine the contents of one's credit records. Consumer reports are known to have a high incidence of inaccurate, incomplete, and misleading information. It has been charged that certain consumer-reporting agencies set quotas of "adverse" reports for their agents—that is, the agent must come up with derogatory information in a certain percentage of his investigations. It has also been charged that some agencies conduct haphazard investigations and fill their reports with a lot of unverified, even invented data, a result of the enormous daily and weekly quotas that each agency investigator is expected to complete.[30] The trouble and expense of obtaining access to one's credit records are well worthwhile if measured against the risk of needlessly losing a job or loan or insurance policy.

Can anything be done if the information in a credit record is inaccurate?

Yes.

Under the FCRA, if an item appears to be inaccurate or incomplete, the subject may so inform the agency, and the agency must reinvestigate the item within a "reasonable period of time." However, the agency may refuse to reinvestigate if it believes the dispute to be "frivolous" or "irrelevant." [31] The act does not specify just what such reinvestigation entails: in practice, it may turn out to be no more than a renewed query to the original source of the information. (Under the Maine statute, which has the most stringent provisions for reinvestigations, the agency must note in the record what steps it took to reinvestigate a disputed item.[32]) Nor does the FCRA define how an agency may decide to dismiss a request as "frivolous," except to say that the mere presence of contradictory information in the record "does not in and of itself constitute reasonable grounds" for such a judgment.[33] Obviously, a great deal of scope is left to the agency's discretion.

If the agency cannot verify the disputed information, it is supposed to delete it from the records. If no such correction is made, the subject may enter into the record a brief statement of his own version of the story, and in subsequent disseminations of the information, the fact that the item is in dispute must be clearly noted and the subject's statement or a summary of it must be included. But again, if the agency considers the dispute "frivolous," it may refuse to accept the statement into the record. The agency may limit the statement to 100 words if it helps the person write a clear summary of the dispute.[34]

The subject also has the right to demand that previous recipients of the disputed information be informed of the correction or be given the explanatory statement. The agency must, at minimum, inform any person who received the disputed information for employment purposes within the last two years, or for any other purpose within the last six months.[35] The agency may not charge a fee for notifying previous recipients of an item that was found to be inaccurate or could not be verified, nor for transmitting to such recipients the subject's explanatory statement, if he has suffered an "adverse action" based on a consumer report within the last thirty days. In other circumstances, a fee may be charged, so long as the subject is told ahead of time what the fee will be.[36]

Can a consumer-reporting agency be sued for invading a person's privacy, for disseminating false or damaging information, or for violating a person's rights under a fair-credit-reporting statute?

Yes, but with difficulty.

Under the federal statute, a consumer-reporting agency, the user of a report, or a person furnishing information for a report may be sued for defamation, invasion of privacy, or negligence only with respect to "false information furnished with malice or willful intent to injure." [37] Because it is very difficult to prove actual malice and willful intent, such suits are extremely hard to win. The only state statutes that do not effectively immunize agencies, users, and sources from defamation and invasion-of-privacy suits are those in Montana, Maine, and New York.[38]

The FCRA permits suits against a consumer-reporting agency or report user for willful noncompliance or negligent noncompliance with any requirement of the act. In the case of willful noncompliance, the injured person may be awarded actual damages, punitive damages, and costs and attorneys' fees.[39] For negligent noncompliance, the court may award actual damages and costs and attorneys' fees.[40] The obstacle here is that reporting agencies and users can defend against negligence suits by demonstrating that they took "reasonable procedures" to comply with the statute. Because the act does not define or specify any "reasonable procedures," the showing of a "good faith effort" on the part of the agency may be enough for a successful defense.

Civil suits under the FCRA may be brought in a U.S. district court or other court of competent jurisdiction. There is a two-year statute of limitations. However, when a defendant reporting agency or report user has willfully misrepresented information, and when that information is material to the case against the agency or user, the two-year period does not begin until the discovery of the misrepresentation.[41]

Though damage suits under the federal and most state acts can be difficult, successful litigation is by no means impossible. The first and best-known award of damages under the FCRA to the victim of a prejudicial consumer report was *Millstone* v. *O'Hanlon Reports* (1974). James Millstone's automobile-insurance policy was canceled after the insurance company received a consumer report characterizing him as a hippie and a suspected drug user. The accusation had been made by a former—soon afterwards deceased—neighbor. The reporting agency made no attempt to verify the information and repeatedly denied Millstone access to his records. An outraged court, calling the agency's methods "slipshod and slovenly," awarded Millstone $25,000 punitive damages, $2500 actual damages, and $12,500 for costs and attorneys' fees. The award was upheld on appeal against the agency's claim that its information practices were protected by the First Amendment.[42]

Millstone obviously set an important precedent for the victims of similarly egregious violations of the FCRA.[43] There have been other, less spectacular victories which are also encouraging. For example, in a settlement by stipulation (a court-supervised agreement between the parties), a woman whose auto insurance was canceled because of a report that she was living with a man "without benefit of wedlock" obtained an acknowledgment from the insurance company that it had improperly denied her a policy, and the deletion of the item from her credit records. The stipulation also contained an instruction from the insurer to the credit-reporting agency not to include any "moral judgments" about the relationships among the people in a household in any future report.[44] Negligent noncompliance was found in another case in which a credit bureau did not bother to establish an exact match of name and address in reporting a civil suit against a particular individual, who turned out not to be the person actually involved in the suit.[45] There have been several cases which suggest that recovery may be possible where agencies have reported "adverse information" without taking reasonable measures to discover and report the surrounding, possibly mitigating circumstances (for example, the fact that a "bad debt" was really the result of a dispute between creditor and debtor over the validity of the bill).[46]

Nevertheless, anyone contemplating a civil suit for violation of the federal and state fair-credit-reporting statutes must be forewarned that the laws do not place vindication or restitution within easy reach.

What other laws regulate credit reports?

The Equal Credit Opportunity Act [47] prohibits credit grantors from using a person's race, sex, marital status, and certain other potentially discriminatory standards in making decisions on the extension of loans or credit. This does not necessarily mean that such items won't continue to be noted in a person's credit records, however, since the law forbids only their use by the creditor, not their collection by a consumer-reporting agency.

The Fair Credit Billing Act [48] forbids the reporting of a disputed bill as a "delinquent account" for the ninety days during which a person may withhold a disputed payment. This does have a direct effect on credit records, because the notation of a delinquency in a consumer report usually results in the refusal of further credit. The statute requires that such accounts be reported as disputed, or, after ninety days, as both disputed and delinquent; within the ninety-day period, no creditor may use a disputed account as grounds for refusing credit or a loan.

Both the Equal Credit Opportunity Act and the Fair Credit Billing Act apply only to the uses of information by creditors. Neither places restrictions on employers, insurers, or other consumer-report users.

NOTES

1. Privacy Protection Study Commission, Personal Privacy in an Information Society 325–26 (U.S. Government Printing Office, July 1977).
2. Id. 55–56.
3. 15 U.S.C. 1681 et seq.
4. 15 U.S.C. 1681a.
5. 16 C.F.R. 600.6.
6. Beresh v. Retail Credit Co., 358 F. Supp. 260 (C.D. Cal., 1973).

7. BUREAU OF CONSUMER PROTECTION, DIVISION OF CONSUMER CREDIT, FEDERAL TRADE COMMISSION, COMPLIANCE WITH THE FAIR CREDIT REPORTING ACT 46–47 (2nd ed. rev., January 1977).

8. Rasor v. Retail Credit Co., 554 P.2d 1041 (Wash., 1976).

9. Peller v. Retail Credit Co., 359 F. Supp. 1235 (N.D.Ga., 1973); aff'd 505 F.2d 733 (5th Cir., 1974).

10. 15 U.S.C. 1681e(b). The best-known case addressing the definition of "reasonable procedures" is Miller v. Credit Bureau, No. SC–29451–71, CCH Consumer Credit Guide, Par. 99, 173 (D.C. Super. Ct., 1972).

11. 15 U.S.C. 1681c.

12. N.Y. GEN. BUS. LAW §380; ME. REV. STAT. ANN. tit. 10, §1312.

13. See CAL. CIV. CODE §§1785–1786; N.M. STAT. ANN. §§50–8–1 et seq.; KY. REV. STAT. §331.350.

14. E.g., there are numerous statutes and regulations restricting persons to whom arrest and conviction records, medical records, school records, etc., may be released. However, pretext interviews—in which the interviewer misrepresents his identity or the purpose of the interview—are not now illegal.

15. 15 U.S.C. 1681d.

16. 15 U.S.C. 1681m(a).

17. 15 U.S.C. 1681m(b).

18. 15 U.S.C. 1681f.

19. 15 U.S.C. 1681e(a).

20. 15 U.S.C. 1681q.

21. 15 U.S.C. 1681r.

22. 15 U.S.C. 1681g.

23. See, e.g., OKLA. STAT. ANN. tit. 24, §§81–85; MD. COM. LAW §§14–1201 et seq.; ARIZ. REV. STAT. ANN. §§44–1691 et seq.; N.Y. GEN. BUS. LAW, supra note 12; ME. REV. STAT. ANN. supra note 12; CAL. CIV. CODE, supra note 13.

24. 15 U.S.C. 1681g(a)(1).

25. 15 U.S.C. 1681g(a)(2).

26. 15 U.S.C. 1681g(a)(3).

27. 15 U.S.C. 1681h(a) and (b).

28. 15 U.S.C. 1681h(c).

29. 15 U.S.C. 1681j.

30. Privacy Protection Study Commission, supra note 1, Chapter 8.

31. 15 U.S.C. 1681i(a).

32. ME. REV. STAT. ANN., supra note 12.

33. 15 U.S.C. 1681i(a).

34. 15 U.S.C. 1681i(a), (b), and (c).

35. 15 U.S.C. 1681i(d).

36. 15 U.S.C. 1681j.

37. 15 U.S.C. 1681h(e).
38. MONT. REV. CODES ANN. §§18–501 *et seq.;* ME. REV. STAT. ANN., *supra* note 12; N.Y. GEN. BUS. LAW, *supra* note 12.
39. 15 U.S.C. 1681n.
40. 15 U.S.C. 1681o.
41. 15 U.S.C. 1681p.
42. 383 F. Supp. 269 (D.C.Mo., 1974); 528 F.2d 829 (8th Cir., 1976).
43. *E.g., see also* Rasor v. Retail Credit Co., *supra* note 8; Collins v. Retail Credit Co., 410 F. Supp. 924 (D.C.Mich., 1976).
44. Cranz v. State Farm, Civ. Action No. 1858–73 (D.N.J., 1975).
45. King v. Credit Bureau of Georgia, 4 CCH Consumer Credit Guide, Par. 98, 635 (D.D.C., March 12, 1975).
46. *E.g.,* Miller v. Credit Bureau, *supra* note 10; Green v. Stores Mutual Protective Association, 74 Civ. 4607 (S.D. N.Y., October 7, 1975).
47. 15 U.S.C. 1691.
48. 15 U.S.C. 1666–1666j.

V

Criminal-Justice Records

Which agencies keep arrest and conviction records?

All of the agencies that constitute the criminal-justice system keep records of arrests and convictions: police, prosecutors, courts, probation departments, prisons, parole boards, and the many subsidiary agencies that serve each of these.

In addition, the Federal Bureau of Investigation maintains records with arrest and conviction information submitted by local, state, and federal agencies. A federal statute authorizes the FBI, as the agent of the Attorney General, to "acquire, collect, classify, and preserve identification, criminal identification, crime, and other records" and to "exchange these records with, and for the official use of, authorized officials of the federal government, the states, cities, and penal and other institutions." [1] Under that authority, the FBI maintains information about individuals who have been arrested on a document known as an identification record, commonly referred to as a "rap sheet." The rap sheet identifies the contributor (the local, state, or federal agency that provided the information), the name and physical description of the subject, the date and charge of each arrest, and (sometimes, but not always) dispositions. The FBI asserts that it is merely the custodian of the information on the rap sheet, and disclaims responsibility for the accuracy or completeness of the records it maintains.

Similar identification and criminal-history repositories exist in many states, some computerized, others manual. Like the FBI, most of these repositories rely totally upon the diligence of contributing agencies, such as local police departments and courts, to submit complete, timely, and accurate information. When contributing agencies are careless or slow in providing information on arrests and dispositions, the rap sheets will be unreliable. In fact, it has been found that both the FBI and the state repositories disseminate significant quantities of incorrect or incomplete records. Yet the police and the courts frequently rely upon these records to guide their actions in questioning suspects, making arrests, setting bail, fashioning strategy for prosecutions and plea bargains, imposing sentences. When the records become available outside the criminal-justice system, they are used, most frequently by employers, to make important decisions that profoundly affect people's lives.

Are arrest and conviction records confidential?

Not really. Federal regulations provide only minimal confidentiality. Although many states have statutes or regulations supposedly protecting the confidentiality of criminal-justice records, most are vague or inadequate in significant respects.

The federal Law Enforcement Assistance Administration (LEAA) has issued regulations governing the privacy and security of certain criminal-justice records.[2] The LEAA regulations apply to the FBI and to state and local agencies that have received LEAA funds for the collection, storage, and dissemination of criminal-history records in either manual or automated systems since July 1, 1973. Because LEAA financial assistance has been given to almost all state and local criminal-justice record systems, most systems around the country are subject to these regulations. But because the LEAA regulations apply only to limited categories of criminal-justice records and contain many exemptions, their practical effect is limited.

First, the regulations apply only to "criminal history record information," which is defined to consist of notations of arrest, detention, indictment or other formal criminal charges, and any disposition stemming from those charges (including, for example, dismissal or sentencing).[3] Criminal-history record information does not include, and therefore the LEAA regulations do not govern, the following:

1. "wanted" posters;
2. original records of entry (such as police arrest books

or "blotters") that are compiled chronologically
and required by law or long-standing custom to be
made public;
3. court records;
4. opinions in public judicial proceedings;
5. records of traffic offenses maintained for licensing
purposes;
6. announcements of executive clemency;
7. fingerprint records compiled for use outside the
criminal-justice system, such as background checks
for employment in public agencies.[4]

Even with respect to data defined as criminal-history
record information, the LEAA regulations place no limit
on dissemination to criminal-justice agencies in any jurisdiction for criminal-justice purposes, including employment within the criminal-justice system.[5]

Furthermore, the regulations place no limits on the
dissemination of criminal-history information about an
offense for which an individual is currently within the
jurisdiction of the criminal-justice system.[6] For the purposes of this provision, a person is within the system at
any time from arrest through incarceration, and including
parole, probation, or other court-ordered supervision.
Moreover, when an agency possesses incomplete records
and can obtain no current information indicating whether
a person is still within the criminal-justice system, it may
assume that a person is within the system for a period of
one year following the date of arrest.

The LEAA regulations place no limits on the dissemination of conviction information.[7] Unless sealed or otherwise
restricted by state law, conviction records can be disseminated to almost anyone. (See the explanation of
sealing statutes later in this chapter.)

Thus, the only real restrictions imposed by the LEAA
regulations are upon the dissemination of "nonconviction
data" to public or private agencies that are not a part of
the criminal-justice system. "Nonconviction data" include
criminal-history information when the arrest charges were
not referred for prosecution, were dismissed, or resulted
in an acquittal. In addition, the category is defined to
cover records of arrests more than a year old that are

unaccompanied by disposition information and for which no prosecution is actively pending.[8]

The regulations provide that nonconviction data may be disseminated only to:

1. criminal-justice agencies for criminal-justice and employment purposes;
2. public and private agencies authorized by state or federal statute, executive order, local ordinance, or court decision to receive them;
3. private individuals and agencies acting under contract to a criminal-justice agency to provide criminal-justice services;
4. agencies engaged in evaluative or statistical research.[9]

A few states have enacted restrictions on the contents and dissemination of criminal-justice records that go beyond the limits of the LEAA regulations. Iowa, for example, has a comprehensive statute restricting the dissemination of certain kinds of criminal-history information and forbidding altogether the maintenance of any noncriminal "surveillance" data, while Minnesota forbids the dissemination of "private or confidential" data to Interpol, the private international police agency.[10] But given all the exceptions of the LEAA regulations, and the failure of most states to legislate in this area, it cannot be said that the personal data in criminal-justice records are confidential in any practical sense.

Do people have a right to see their own arrest and conviction records?

Yes. A person's access to his own criminal-justice records is governed by federal and state regulations, and in some states, by statute.

A person may obtain a copy of his FBI rap sheet by writing directly to the FBI Identification Division, Washington, D.C. 20537. The request must be accompanied by name, date and place of birth, and a set of "rolled-ink fingerprint impressions" taken upon standard fingerprint cards. A set of fingerprints can be most simply obtained at a local police station upon request.[11]

Each request for an FBI rap sheet must be accompanied by a $5 fee in the form of a certified check or money order payable to the Treasurer of the United States. A person may request a waiver of the fee based upon a claim of indigency. An indigency application may be made merely by enclosing a brief letter explaining the reasons why one is unable to pay the fee. If the letter is not acceptable to the FBI, it will usually advise the writer of the problem and give him the opportunity to submit additional information. The FBI will consider, but need not grant, a request to waive the fee.

The rap sheet maintained by state repositories do not necessarily duplicate rap sheets maintained by FBI. Often there will be significant differences in the information maintained on a person by several different repositories. A person who wishes to inspect his rap sheet is well advised to check both the FBI and the repository of any state in which an arrest took place.

A few states provide a right of access to one's own criminal-history records by statute.[12] LEAA regulations require that individuals be given the right of access to their rap sheets in any record system assisted with LEAA funds, although the scope of the right and the procedures for exercising it vary from system to system. A telephone call to the criminal-records division of local police headquarters should be all that is necessary to determine what procedure must be followed in one's own state. However, records of arrests and convictions that occurred in other states will seldom be compiled on the rap sheet in one's home state; it is therefore necessary to ask for one's rap sheet from the repository of every state in which an arrest or conviction took place. (Again, a telephone call to the criminal-records division of a police department in each of these other states should elicit the necessary instructions for obtaining a rap sheet.)

It is worth repeating this admonition: because the consequences of the use of arrest and conviction information both within the community of criminal-justice agencies and outside it—especially by employers—can be so serious, anyone who has ever been arrested or convicted should check his rap sheets wherever they are stored, in state repositories as well as the FBI. In spite of the trouble and expense, it is important to find out what information the rap sheets contain, to make sure they are complete and correct, and, whenever possible, to seal them or take other steps to prevent their further dissemination.

May a rap sheet be corrected if it contains inaccurate or incomplete information?

Yes.

FBI regulations provide that if an individual believes his FBI rap sheet is inaccurate or incomplete, correction or updating of the information must be requested by the police department or other criminal-justice agency that contributed the information to the FBI.[13] The FBI will make such changes as are directed by the contributing agency.

Getting a contributing agency to forward a rap-sheet correction to the FBI can be something of an ordeal. Over-burdened or uninterested police officials may simply not want to be bothered, and the burden of proof to sub-stantiate the correction—for example, by producing a copy of a court record showing the disposition of an arrest —is usually upon the subject of the record. However, the stakes are well worth the effort: it can be very significant, if one has a later encounter with the police or the courts, to show that an earlier arrest actually ended in the dis-missal of charges or acquittal. (Disposition information is the most frequently missing or incorrect item.) People who experience difficulties in correcting a record often find they need a lawyer's help, although it can be done alone, with persistance and determination.

It is a good idea to ask the police department or other contributing agency to forward a correction to the state repository as well as to the FBI—in fact, anyplace else where the original record was sent. Procedures for correc-tion under state statutes or regulations, where they exist, are often similar to those of the FBI, and require the correction to be made by the contributing agency.

Local legal-aid and legal-services societies and ex-offender organizations are good sources of information about the procedures to be followed for the correction of a rap sheet in any particular state or locality.

May an arrest or conviction record be sealed or ex-punged?

Under some circumstances.

Nearly half the states provide for the sealing or ex-pungement (erasing) of certain arrest or conviction rec-ords by statute. The statutes cover different kinds of records and different sets of circumstances, and require various procedures to be initiated by record subjects, the courts, or the state record repository. In New York, for example, records of arrests not resulting in conviction are supposed to be sealed automatically, and fingerprints and mug shots returned to the subject. In Massachusetts, a convicted person can petition the court that had jurisdiction of the case to seal the record of a felony conviction after ten years, or a misdemeanor conviction after five. In Maryland, the record of an arrest not followed by conviction, or a conviction followed by a sentence of probation, can be expunged upon the defendant's petition to the court.[14]

But state sealing and expungement statutes have many loopholes. Often, a sealed or even supposedly expunged record remains available for certain purposes: it may be reopened by petition of a prosecutor to a court, for example, or disclosed to gun-licensing or law-enforcement agencies. In some jurisdictions, sealed records may not really be sealed or physically sequestered at all, but merely stamped with the word "sealed" or placed in a separate but open file. Sealing or expungement may be barred totally if the person was ever convicted of a crime in any other jurisdiction. The sealing procedure may have to be initiated by the defendant, and many defendants remain unaware of their right to seek such relief. In some states, a defendant's petition to seal can be denied if the prosecutor claims that the record should remain open "in the interests of justice."[15] Legal-services and ex-offender organizations can provide information on the sealing procedures available in the various states that have sealing or expungement laws.

Where there are no statutes allowing the sealing or expungement of a record, the courts have occasionally stepped in to provide relief to a person who wishes to have an arrest or conviction record destroyed. A milestone decision ordering the destruction of an FBI rap sheet was *Menard* v. *Saxbe*,[16] in which the court stressed the stigma and the potential serious harm to an individual in the continued maintenance and possible dissemination of an inaccurate record. In another important case, the court ordered the destruction of the arrest records of 13,000

persons who were illegally arrested during the 1971 antiwar Mayday demonstrations in Washington, D.C.[17]

A lawsuit to expunge or even to correct a record can
be very difficult. If there is no statutory or regulatory
remedy, it is possible that a court will provide relief where
an arrest was clearly illegal, or where it can be demonstrated that the likely harm to the individual in the dissemination of the records (such as to employers) outweighs
the "compelling interest of law enforcement" in maintaining the record. Yet would-be litigants should be cautioned
by the decision of the U.S. Supreme Court in *Paul* v. *Davis*
in 1976,[18] which held that the wide public circulation of
an arrest record—an erroneous record at that—by police
officials did not violate the right of privacy or any other
constitutional right.

May employers obtain access to arrest and conviction records?

Yes, and they frequently do.

Criminal-justice record systems governed by LEAA regulations are permitted to disseminate conviction records
to anyone, including employers. While the regulations appear to deny employers access to records of arrests not
followed by conviction, they are vague enough to allow
such access unless a state statute, regulation, or court
ruling explicitly forbids it. A few states—notably California, Illinois, Massachusetts, and New York—forbid employers to ask applicants about arrests that did not result
in conviction.[19] But almost everywhere, some or all public
agencies may (or even must) check the arrest as well as
conviction records of employment applicants, and many
state occupational-licensing laws require such a check.
After law-enforcement agencies, employers are the major
users of criminal-justice records, and an arrest history,
even without conviction, is one of the most common factors in employment discrimination.

(See also Chapter VIII on employment records, for a
discussion of waivers permitting employers to check arrest
records, and Chapter IV for a discussion of the part
played by credit-reporting agencies in disseminating arrest
and conviction information to employers.)

Are juvenile arrest and conviction records confidential?

Juvenile records are purportedly made confidential by statute in every state. Many states provide procedures by which a juvenile record may be sealed or expunged upon the individual's eighteenth or twenty-first birthday. Nonetheless, records of juvenile arrests and convictions (sometimes called "adjudications of delinquency," in the parlance of the juvenile court) are widely disseminated among criminal-justice agencies, and also beyond—to social-services agencies, schools, clinics, and other agencies or institutions that deal with juveniles. In practice, it is not terribly difficult to obtain access to juvenile arrest and conviction records.[20]

One of the most serious problems faced by a person who has a juvenile record is the possibility that it will be discovered by prospective employers. Employers frequently circumvent the statutory barriers that deny them direct access to juvenile records simply by demanding that applicants reveal any juvenile arrests or convictions. While the applicant may be tempted to lie, he knows that the employer may reject him later for dishonesty if the truth comes out. In fact, applications for many jobs with government agencies, and even with some private employers, state specifically that submission of false information on the application will be treated as sufficient reason for rejection or dismissal. There is no answer to this dilemma, so long as employers are virtually unrestricted in the questions they may ask applicants.

NOTES

1. 28 U.S.C. 534.
2. 28 C.F.R. 20.
3. 28 C.F.R. 20.3(b).
4. 28 C.F.R. 20.20(b) and 20.3(b).
5. 28 C.F.R. 20.21(b)(1).
6. 28 C.F.R. 20.21(c).
7. 28 C.F.R. 20.21(b).
8. 28 C.F.R. 20.3(k).
9. 28 C.F.R. 20.21(b)(1)–(4).
10. IOWA CODE ANN. §749B.1; MINN. STAT. ANN. §15.1643.
11. 28 C.F.R. 16.30.
12. *See, e.g.,* ALASKA STAT. §12.62.010; ARK. STAT. ANN. §5–

1109; CAL PENAL CODE §§11075-81; GA. CODE ANN. §92A–30006; IOWA CODE ANN., *supra* note 10; ME. REV. STAT. ANN. tit. 16, §606; VA. CODE §9–111.3.

13. 28 C.F.R. 16.30.
14. N.Y. CRIM. PROC. LAW, §160.50; MASS. ANN. LAWS ch. 276, §§100A–C; MD. ANN. CODE art. 27, §§735–741.
15. *E.g.,* N.Y. CRIM. PROC. LAW, *supra* note 14.
16. 498 F.2d 1017 (D.C.Cir., 1974).
17. Sullivan v. Murphy, 478 F.2d 938 (D.C. Cir., 1973); *cert. denied,* 414 U.S. 880 (1974).
18. 424 U.S. 693 (1976).
19. CAL. LAB. CODE §432.7; ILL. REV. STAT. ch. 48, §853; MASS. ANN. LAWS, *supra* note 14; N.Y. CORREC. LAW §§750 *et seq.*
20. *See* ALAN SUSSMAN, THE RIGHTS OF YOUNG PEOPLE 108–112 (Avon 1977).

VI

Social-Services Records

What kinds of information are contained in social-services records?

Every kind of personal information imaginable.

Social-services records are the personal records maintained by government agencies that dispense cash or services to financially needy persons. Welfare is one form of such assistance. So are food stamps, Medicaid, housing subsidies, employment training, family-planning services, drug- or alcohol-abuse treatment, day care, legal services, rehabilitative services for the handicapped, and dozens of other programs that administer publicly funded assistance and services free or at low cost to people who are in need. The clients of such programs are primarily the poor, but not exclusively; many middle-class people are the beneficiaries of one or another social-services program at some time in their lives.

Social-services and welfare records contain all of the personal information that is initially gathered to determine and verify a client's eligibility for benefits, descriptions of the services and benefits dispensed to the client, and the accumulation of data recording the course of the client's relationship with the agency. In addition to objective data, such records may contain the judgments and observations of agency personnel about a client's character or attitudes. Information about the client's family is frequently included, even though other family members are not receiving benefits. Certain types of records may contain highly sensitive information: the client's personal confidences to a counselor in a drug-treatment program, for example, or confessions of criminal offenses to a legal-services attorney.

Because publicly funded social-services programs run

the gamut of human experience and problems, so too do the records they generate.

Must welfare clients and other recipients of government assistance reveal all their personal records in order to establish eligibility for benefits?

Generally, yes. Clients are required not only to produce records in their own possession but also to waive the confidentiality of records held by third parties.

Welfare and other social-services agencies establish and verify client eligibility primarily by collecting detailed personal information. Subjects covered include clients' finances and possessions, education, employment, criminal history, physical and mental health, family and social relationships, use of drugs and alcohol, sometimes even the intimacies of their sex lives and use of contraceptives. There is no practical way for a prospective client to withhold any of this information from an assistance agency without seriously jeopardizing his efforts to obtain benefits. The client is forced to allow deep intrusions into his personal life as the price for receiving government help.

To establish eligibility for most public assistance and social-services programs, the client must sign a waiver of confidentiality permitting the administering agency to examine all his bank, tax, medical, employment, and similar personal records, to exchange information with other agencies that have served the client, and to talk with neighbors, employers, and personal acquaintances. Although other chapters of this book suggest methods by which readers might avoid or at least narrow the scope of such "blanket waivers," there is little chance that the individual public-assistance or social-services client, acting independently, can successfully do so.

While clients cannot resist most government intrusions into their personal lives and records, there are established procedures whereby the discriminatory or unfair *use* of certain information to make a decision about a client can be challenged. These procedures vary according to the program in question and the jurisdiction—federal state, or local—in which it is administered. Local welfare-rights and legal-services organizations can advise a client of the hearing rights available in a particular social-services or welfare program.

Must recipients of assistance allow agency officials into their homes?

Yes. Caseworkers may visit recipients in their homes and conduct "reasonable" searches to assess the client's living conditions. But the Supreme Court has outlawed such "unreasonable" searches as middle-of-the-night surprise visits.[1]

May clients see and correct their records?

Frequently not. Despite the obvious hardships and injustices that result when an agency does not have accurate, timely, complete, and relevant records upon which to base its eligibility judgments, most welfare and social-services programs do not provide formal client rights of access and correction.

There are some exceptions. When a client has requested a hearing to challenge an agency's decision, he is often allowed to examine at least those documents and records the agency will use at the hearing. Clients of the federally funded, state-administered Aid to Families with Dependent Children (AFDC), Medicaid, and Title XX Social Services programs have the right, preparatory to a hearing, to examine their complete case files.[2] Any social-services programs administered directly by a federal agency, such as the Supplemental Security Income program of the Social Security Administration, are subject to client rights of access and correction under the Privacy Act of 1974 [3] (see Chapters XIV and XV). Records held by state welfare and social-services agencies may be open to clients where there is an analogous state privacy act.

However, there are many state and local programs that do not permit client access under any conditions. Moreover, even in those programs in which clients have a right of access preparatory to a hearing, the client who has no grounds for a hearing but merely wishes to inspect his records, to see what is there and whether it is correct, usually has no means of doing so.

With or without formal procedures for access, individual caseworkers will sometimes give the client the chance to review his own records. The client should always explore this possibility. If a request is refused by the caseworker, local welfare-rights or legal-services organizations can offer guidance to the availability of rights of access and correction in specific welfare and social-services programs.

May agencies disclose information from case records without a client's permission?

Usually, yes.

Most welfare and social-services programs are subject to statutes or regulations that require, in general terms, that the confidentiality of client records must be protected. These requirements, however, are hedged by vague language and numerous exceptions. For example, an agency is nearly always permitted to make disclosures "necessary to provide service to the individual" or "for purposes directly connected to the program." Such standards allow disclosures not only to other agencies presently serving the client, but also to agencies that may serve the client in the future, even when he has not initiated an application. Many states, as well as counties, localities, and federal agencies, operate central "human services" databanks to which client records are submitted for virtually permanent storage. Police and other criminal-justice officials can often obtain information from client records simply on request. Schools, employers, and landlords are sometimes told that a student, employee, or tenant is the client of a welfare or social-services program. Records are often made available to researchers. So loose are the confidentiality regulations for most programs that these disclosures are perfectly legal.

On the other hand, some programs maintain a very strict confidentiality; for example, federally funded drug- and alcohol-abuse-treatment programs generally protect client records even against a subpoena.[4]

Disclosures of client records often occur under procedures designed to combat fraud—to catch "welfare cheats." Government auditors are frequently empowered to examine individual client records to insure that both eligibility determinations and provision of services are in accordance with applicable law and regulations. On a larger scale are audits implemented by computer matches of separate record systems; for example, the matching of the names of welfare clients against employment rolls to find welfare recipients who are earning money in violation of eligibility rules. Inspired by the federal government's

Project Match, launched in 1977, which matched the federal payroll against local welfare rolls, many states and localities are instituting similar computerized record-matching operations involving both public and private payrolls.

Except where client records are directly subject to the confidentiality provisions of the federal Privacy Act or a state privacy act, the welfare or social-services client has no meaningful legal "expectation of privacy," and no practical recourse when a disclosure is made without his permission.

What is the Parent Locator Service?

It is a record-searching operation implementing the Child Support Enforcement Program under Title IV-D of the Social Security Act.[5] Its purpose is to locate the absent fathers of children receiving AFDC benefits, and to collect child-support payments from them as a full or partial substitute for public assistance. The federal government gives special grants to states that establish child-support enforcement agencies and parent-locator services; in addition, the federal government itself operates a Parent Locator Service (PLS) within the Department of Health and Human Services.

Parents who are recipients of AFDC must, as a condition of benefits, cooperate with the PLS to find an absent father. This means that a woman must name the father of her children, cooperate in establishing paternity, and give information that will help to determine his whereabouts. If she refuses, she will lose her benefits, and the benefits for her children will be paid to and administered by a third party. There is a "good-cause" exception, which exempts the mother from these requirements if efforts to locate the missing father would not be in the "best interests" of the child. Such a determination might be made if the child was conceived by rape or incest, or if it is reasonably anticipated that the father would harm the child or the mother, physically or emotionally. But even to establish "good cause," the mother must give information about the identity of the father and the nature of their relationship. In some states, PLS paternity investigations have required women to complete questionnaires revealing all of their sexual relationships, including dates

and places and the names of witnesses, and to take polygraph tests.

The PLS is also available, on a voluntary basis, to parents who are not on welfare, to force an absent father to
pay court-awarded child-support payments.

The PLS is a cooperative federal-state enterprise. Tax,
welfare, motor-vehicle, Post Office, police, in fact any
records of any federal, state, or local government agency
may be searched for clues to the whereabouts of the absent
father, and so may the records of private organizations,
such as employers, unions, and telephone companies. The
key to the search is usually the Social Security number,
which has come to be used as the universal identifier for
all important public and private records.

The authority of a PLS agency to search through records usually overrides any other regulatory or statutory
protections for the confidentiality of records. Except in the
few states that have privacy acts, the confidentiality of the
records compiled by state PLS and child-support enforcement agencies themselves is protected only by agency
regulations. As is the case with so many other social-
services records, these regulations give record subjects no
legally enforceable expectation of confidentiality to protect
them against unauthorized disclosures. It must be emphasized that the subjects of PLS records need not themselves
be public-assistance clients; they need only be named as
an absent parent by a person who is a public-assistance
client.

NOTES

1. Wyman v. James, 400 U.S. 309 (1971).
2. 45 C.F.R. 205.10(a)(13)(i).
3. 5 U.S.C. 552a.
4. 42 C.F.R. 2.1–2.67.
5. 42 U.S.C. 402(a), 454(4), 602(a)(26), 654(4), as
   amended by Pub. L. No. 93–647 and Pub. L. No. 94–88;
   45 C.F.R. 232 and 302.

VII

Medical Records

Doesn't the doctor-patient privilege assure the privacy of medical records?

No.

More than forty states have statutes that protect the confidentiality of communications between physician or psychiatrist and patient—the doctor-patient privilege. But these statutes merely prevent the doctor from being forced to testify about the patient's communications or reveal the patient's records in a court of law without the patient's consent. They have no application to the enormous number of situations in which a physician is permitted or compelled, by law, regulation, or long-established practice, to reveal information about the patient to outside parties.

Even under doctor-patient-privilege statutes, doctors may be required to testify about a patient or reveal a patient's records. In a criminal case, medical testimony may be introduced by the prosecution or the defense. In a civil case—such as a negligence or malpractice suit, a divorce or custody suit, or a commitment proceeding—the medical history and condition of the principals may be the primary questions at issue.[1] In any of these situations, a patient's physician may be required by the court to describe his medical history and even produce his records.

A further restriction upon the reach of privilege statutes is that they apply only in cases governed by state law. The Federal Rules of Evidence, which govern practice in federal courts, provide only a psychotherapist-patient privilege, not a general doctor-patient privilege. Under the Federal Rules, communications between physician and patient may be revealed at the discretion of the court, guided in its judgment by "the principles of the common law as they may be interpreted by the courts of the United States in the light of reason and experience." Where state law is applicable to a case, the privilege is determined "in accordance with the state law." [2]

Though the words "doctor-patient privilege" are often used rhetorically to describe the principle of confidentiality that is popularly attributed to the relationship between doctor and patient, the privilege is in reality a narrowly drawn rule of evidence, not even recognized in the common law (as is, for example, the attorney-client privilege), but available only where it is specifically provided by statute.

To whom do doctors and hospitals commonly reveal patients' records?

The following is just a partial list, noting only the most common recipients of information and records.

Insurance companies. Both to establish an applicant's eligibility for health, life, and disability policies and to process claims under such policies, insurance companies require extensive medical information from the patient's physicians and psychiatrists and from his hospital records. So much medical information is collected by insurance companies, in fact, that the industry maintains its own giant medical databank, called the Medical Information Bureau.

Government service payers. The government agencies that finance and administer Medicare, Medicaid, Social Security disability, and workmen's-compensation programs all require the submission of patient treatment records as a prerequisite for authorizing payments. State and federal agencies that administer special publicly funded medical services, such as treatment for drug addiction and alcoholism, mental-health problems, and physical handicaps, frequently require access to or information from the patient's records.

Welfare agencies. The many government agencies involved in the administration of welfare and social-services programs often require detailed information about their clients' medical problems and treatment.

Professional accrediting agencies and review boards. Both public and private agencies use patient records to evaluate the quality of professional services provided by doctors and health-care facilities.

Researchers. Many medical-research projects use patient records. Usually, the information can be provided to researchers in aggregate statistical form, but some projects utilize individual, identifiable patient records.

Employers. Applicants for employment are often asked to fill out extensive medical questionnaires and in addition to give prospective employers authorization to see their physician and hospital records. Both applicants and current employees may be required to undergo examinations by company doctors. Employers also obtain diagnostic and treatment information about their employees through claims submitted under company-provided insurance plans.

Credit-reporting agencies. Private credit-reporting agencies compile medical histories and claims investigations for employers and insurance companies, frequently containing information taken directly from physician and hospital records.

Public-health and law-enforcement agencies. Many state laws require hospitals, physicians, and other health-care providers to report certain kinds of diseases, injuries, and treatments to a public-health department or even directly to the police. These may include venereal disease, drug abuse, suspected incidents of child abuse, gunshot wounds, a long list of contagious and epidemic diseases such as typhoid and scarlet fever, abortions, and prescriptions for certain kinds of drugs. Government agencies, such as the National Institute for Occupational Safety and Health, generally can obtain access to employees' health records to use in studies of environmental and occupational hazards. Police departments frequently receive access to medical records in the course of criminal investigations.

Licensing agencies. State occupational-licensing requirements usually include the submission of medical and psychiatric records.

Institutions. When medical services are provided in an institutional setting, such as a school or college, prison, or the armed services, nonmedical personnel within the institution may have access to a patient's records.

Databanks. As a routine adjunct to many of the uses of medical records just described, computerized registries or databanks of particular kinds of patients are maintained by a variety of public and private agencies, from state and local governments to insurance companies and national charities. There are, for example, registries of patients receiving certain prescription drugs, abortion patients, cancer patients, handicapped persons, psychiatric patients, drug addicts, and clients of state-financed medical services. Such patients are seldom even aware that these databanks exist.

The potential dangers of medical databanks have not been recognized, or even closely scrutinized, by the courts. In fact, in a unanimous decision in 1977, the U.S. Supreme Court found no impairment of the right of personal privacy in a state-operated computerized index containing the names of all patients in the state for whom certain "dangerous legitimate drugs" were prescribed. The disclosure of such information to employees of· the New York State Department of Health, said the Court (with surely unintended irony), is not "meaningfully distinguishable from a host of other unpleasant invasions of privacy that are associated with many facets of health care." [3]

Can't patients prevent doctors and hospitals from disclosing their records?

For all practical purposes, no.

In the case of insurance companies and government agencies that reimburse medical services, the patient routinely authorizes the release of his records in a blanket waiver or general consent, which must be signed as a condition of receiving a policy or reimbursement on a claim. Except in California,[4] the waiver does not specify the particular records to be sought, or the particular doctors and hospitals to be contacted, nor does it ordinarily provide an expiration date beyond which the consent is invalid. In fact, some waivers cover not only the signatory but also all other members of his family. Having signed a waiver, the patient has little leverage to resist the company's or government's demands for his records. Occasionally, a particularly alert doctor or hospital-records administrator will balk at what he or she feels to be an excessive demand, such as for the complete patient record rather than information directly pertinent to a claim, or for the details of a psychiatric diagnosis and prognosis. But here, the initiative for protecting a patient's privacy lies with the practitioner or hospital. There is little that the patient himself can do.

It is extremely difficult for a job applicant to resist an employer's demand for medical information, either on a questionnaire or through access to his doctor and hospital records. In most instances, the demand is an implied requirement for consideration of the person's application. There has been little litigation of this issue. In one successful legal challenge to an intrusive preemployment medical inquiry on privacy grounds, a county government was forced to drop questions about applicants' emotional problems, mental-health treatment, use of drugs and alcohol, and "female disorders," to withdraw its blanket release form that forced applicants to authorize county access to all of their medical records, and to pay money damages to an applicant who lost a job because she refused to answer questions she considered offensive.[5]

Most waivers on employment applications, like those on insurance policies, are blanket consents, permitting the employer (or a credit-reporting agency on the employer's behalf) to have access to all of the applicant's medical records. Occasionally, applicants manage at least to limit the effective date of the consent, so that it cannot be reused later. If the employer is going to get medical information through an investigation made by a credit-reporting agency, the applicant might attempt to use his statutory right to be told the "nature and scope" of the investigation [6] as an opportunity to receive a more specific description of the records to be obtained and even to refine the wording of the consent form he must sign (see Chapter IV).

When an applicant or employee is to be examined by a company physician, it is a good idea to ascertain ahead of time what kinds of information the physician will pass along to the employer. Unless he is given explicit assurances of complete confidentiality, the patient should assume that some disclosures will be made to the employer —who is of course the physician's employer too.

Medical records are generally made available for research, accrediting, and professional-review purposes without the patient's knowledge. The laws, regulations, and traditional professional practices governing these functions do not ordinarily include any provision for either notification or consent.[7] Mandatory public-reporting laws, of course, obviate any need for patient consent.

Law-enforcement officers are often able to obtain information from doctors and hospitals informally, simply by announcing that a police investigation is involved. Only the most resolute practitioner or hospital administrator is likely to demand a search warrant or court order before turning over patient records. Again, it is in the hands of the doctor or hospital, not the patient, to decide whether to resist such a demand.

In general, therefore, patients have little opportunity to prevent disclosures of information from their own medical records. The widespread use of the blanket consent form, together with the traditional presumption that medical records "belong" to doctors and hospitals rather than to the individuals whom they describe, conspire to give patients very little direct control over the privacy of their records.

Aren't there any laws restricting disclosures of information by doctors and hospitals?

Yes, but most are riddled with exemptions, and where these specific exemptions do not apply, the laws can easily be circumvented by the routine use of patient waivers.

More than thirty states have statutes restricting access to physician and hospital records in some fashion. Some have a special statute applying to medical or psychiatric records; others simply list medical records as an exempted category in state freedom-of-information laws. Some deal only with medical records in public hospitals and clinics; some apply to both the public and private sectors. But all permit a wide range of disclosures without patient consent, for research, audit, accrediting, investigative, judicial, emergency, and public-health-reporting purposes, and of course permit disclosure with patient consent to insurers, employers, and other interested persons.

In some of the more recently enacted statutes, an attempt has been made to refine the procedures necessary to obtain patient consent. In a 1977 Oregon statute, for example, patient consent to disclosures of medical records held by public hospitals and other public health-care providers must name the agency in which the records are being held, the person or organization to whom disclosure is to be made, the purpose of the disclosure, and the nature and extent of the information to be disclosed. It must be signed and dated by the patient and specify a date or condition of expiration. It may be revoked at any time, even before the stated expiration date.[8] Still, a person whose insurance company or prospective employer demands that he execute such a consent presumably has no realistic choice but to do so.

In addition to state laws that protect the confidentiality of medical records specifically, there are other privacy statutes that can be applied to physician and hospital records. The Privacy Act of 1974, for example, restricts disclosures of medical records held by federal hospitals, the Indian Health Service, the Public Health Service, and other federal health-care facilities.[9] Similar state privacy laws, where they exist, do the same for medical records in clinics, hospitals, and treatment programs run by state and local government agencies. But it must be remembered that the federal act and most of its state analogs provide for disclosures to law-enforcement agencies, and for "routine uses," which can be administratively interpreted to encompass many interagency and outside disclosures for payment, review, research, public-health-reporting, auditing, and investigative purposes. Also, patient waivers can be coerced even under privacy statutes, in that the patient has no effective opportunity to refuse if he wants treatment or reimbursement for treatment. The Family Educational Rights and Privacy Act, dealing with student records, limits the disclosures that school and college medical personnel may make to other persons within or outside the school community without the student's authorization. However, the "health and safety" emergency exceptions to the disclosure prohibitions of both the Family Educational Rights and Privacy Act and the federal

Privacy Act of 1974, as well as analogous state statutes, would frequently apply to disclosures of medical and psychiatric information.[10]

Many federal and state health-care programs are governed by formal regulations that are supposed to prevent disclosures of patient records. Once again, these are usually written to allow many routine disclosures to other government agencies that have some involvement with the patient—welfare departments are a common example—as well as for law-enforcement and research purposes and for entry into various governmental medical databanks, such as abortion, addict, or client-services registries. Disclosures that cannot be accomplished within the regulations can usually be authorized by obtaining the patient's signature on a consent form presented in such a way that the patient has no real choice but to sign.

There is no way to reduce to simple terms the confused tangle of laws and regulations dealing with the privacy of physician and hospital records. A particular patient's records may be subject to any number of overlapping or even conflicting sets of restrictions. But two generalizations—both discouraging—can be made. First, many disclosures from doctor and hospital records to third parties can be made under the terms of existing statutes and regulations, without any need for patient consent or even notification. The patient may not be able to prevent these disclosures, but he should at least try to find out what they are. It is worth taking the time to discuss with one's doctor under what conditions, and for what purposes, he or she would release information to third parties without prior patient authorization. It is also well worth the extra effort necessary to ask the same questions of administrative personnel in the hospitals and clinics where one has received treatment. Such questioning does more than inform the patient; it also puts doctors and hospitals on notice that patients are concerned about their privacy, and thus alerts them to be more careful in making disclosures to outsiders.

The second discouraging generalization is that patient "consent" to a disclosure is often an empty ritual. Such consent is usually demanded in circumstances leaving the patient little choice but to grant it. If there is a choice, patients would do well to ask for very specific information before deciding whether to sign: what records will be released, to whom, for what purpose, what will happen to the records when the purpose is fulfilled, who will have access to them, and for how long. Whenever possible, the consent form should be reworded to reflect all these conditions.

Are there any special legal protections for "sensitive" medical records, like psychiatric or drug-abuse-treament records?

Yes, some. There is, in both law and practice, a growing recognition that many patients will not seek certain kinds of treatment—as for drug and alcohol addiction, venereal disease, mental and emotional problems, abortion, even contraceptive services—if they have to fear the stigma of disclosure.

As noted earlier, many states have statutes granting a privilege to communications between psychiatrists and patients or protecting the confidentiality of mental patients' records, and the Federal Rules of Evidence recognize a psychiatrist-patient privilege. Also as noted earlier, these legislative and judicial safeguards are seriously flawed.

Federal regulations provide special protections for patient records in drug- and alcohol-abuse-treatment programs funded by the federal government.[11] These include tight restrictions on disclosures from patient records even when a subpoena or court order has been served, and prohibit the use of blanket consent forms. The courts themselves have recognized the special sensitivity of addict records. In the best-known judicial test of this issue, New York State's highest court upheld the refusal of the director of a methadone clinic to give the police photographs of all young black male patients in a murder investigation after a witness claimed to have seen the killer at the clinic. The court's judgment in this case, even where there was an admittedly strong public interest in disclosure, shows an appreciation for the paramount importance of the patients' right to privacy.[12]

But there are equally strong pressures in the other direction. A frequent cause of conflict are the attempts by federal or state officials to inspect patient records in the course of an investigation of a treatment facility for irregularities of practice, or even in a routine service audit. Probation and other court officers often ask for information about patients who have been sent into treatment as an alternative to jail. And, of course, many states and localities, and the federal government itself, maintain addict registries that record extensive personal information, often including names or easily decipherable identifiers, about patients in drug-treatment programs. Many of these registries are available for inspection by a variety of state and federal officials.

The privacy of abortion patients has been viewed with scant sympathy by the legislatures and the courts. Many state legislatures have enacted mandatory reporting requirements on abortion patients, often in the form of fetal death certificates, bearing the mother's name, that are preserved for inspection by state officials to serve a variety of auditing, evaluation, research, public-health, and investigative purposes. Such requirements have been upheld, at least in principle, by the U.S. Supreme Court.[13] In fact, even a government computer bank of personally identifiable fetal death certificates survived a constitutional challenge in New York, where the state court of appeals relied on a New York City regulation promising complete confidentiality (except for disclosures to "authorized personnel") of the city's abortion registry as justification for finding no violation of the patients' constitutional right of privacy. It is only small comfort that one of the court's three dissenters noted the "potential for stigmatization" posed by the existence of such a record system in a society in which abortion is still "an emotionally charged" subject.[14]

A different approach to patient privacy is illustrated by the Multi-State Information System (MSIS), a computerized databank in Rockland County, New York, containing detailed patient diagnostic and treatment records submitted by public and private psychiatric-treatment facilities in half a dozen Eastern states and the District of Columbia. To protect these records, the New York State legislature enacted a statute in 1972 immunizing MSIS from demands for access to its records by any official or agency, even under subpoena or court order.[15] Of course, the same records may be available to government officials, with or without a court order, in the local facilities at which MSIS records originate, subject to the vagaries of state law.

All fifty states permit minors to receive treatment for

venereal disease without parental permission. Many also allow minors to have abortions, contraceptive services, or treatment for drug and alcohol addition without their parents' consent. In some states there are statutes specifically forbidding doctors and clinics to disclose such treatment to parents without the child's consent; in others, disclosure is allowed at the discretion of the physician.[16]

Despite the development of special legal protections for some kinds of especially sensitive medical records, patients should be aware that these records are in general no more secure than any other medical records. Insurance companies and government-service payers can still get them; so can researchers, auditors, professional-review committees, welfare agencies, police and other governmental investigators, and even employers. As in so many of the other instances discussed in this chapter, the degree to which the patient's privacy will be protected depends largely on the alertness, discretion, and resolution of the doctor or hospital administrator who maintains the record.

May a patient sue a doctor or hospital that has made an unauthorized disclosure of medical information?

Yes, but the patient should be warned that such suits rarely succeed. The few suits that have succeeded involved either a disclosure that directly and immediately caused a tangible injury to the patient, such as a loss of employment, or actual publication of medical information, in which case the publisher rather than the doctor was frequently the defendant.

A suit for unauthorized disclosure might be formulated on a variety of technical legal grounds: for breach of a contractual relationship between doctor and patient in which the doctor's duty to preserve confidentiality is an implied condition of the contract; for invasion of privacy; for breach of the doctor's fiduciary relationship to the patient; or based on a broad interpretation of state doctor-patient privilege statutes and laws licensing doctors and psychiatrists.[17] If the information disclosed is false, a suit for defamation may be possible.

The odds against the patient in such a suit are formidable. A report on medical records published in 1976 by the National Bureau of Standards explains why. First, patients seldom even know what disclosures have been made, or where, or to whom. Second, lawsuits require a lot of time and money. Third, and most important, a lawsuit means a public trial, bringing further unwanted publicity that only compounds the damage of the original disclosure. And finally, if past experience is any guide, such a lawsuit is virtually impossible to win.[18]

In nearly half the states, a practitioner can have his license revoked for willfully disclosing professional secrets. Confidentiality is an important ethical precept of the medical profession, expressed in the Hippocratic Oath, in the code of ethics of the American Medical Association,[19] and in the codes of many allied health-care professions. Nonetheless, although a physician might risk professional or administrative sanctions for improperly disclosing information about a patient, the patient stands only the most remote chance of winning satisfaction or compensation for himself through the courts.

This generally dismal picture can be expected to improve only if the state legislatures or (preferably) Congress should pass laws giving patients an explicit right of medical confidentiality and a means to enforce that right in the courts. Such statutes, reaching all health-care providers and facilities, would have to delineate clearly the permissible conditions for disclosure without patient consent, and provide an effective civil remedy for violations of the patient's expectation of privacy. Until this happens, patient suits for unauthorized disclosures by doctors and hospitals will remain subject to the vagaries of judicial interpretation, which has generally shown greater deference to the discretion of the doctor than to the expectation of the patient.[20]

Once third parties have obtained medical information from doctors and hospitals, are they legally prevented from making further disclosures?

Only in some circumstances.

Medical information received by a federal agency (perhaps in its capacity as a service payer or employer) is protected by the federal Privacy Act of 1974. In general, this means that a disclosure may be made by the agency without the patient's authorization only for "routine uses" compatible with the agency's lawful administrative function, to a law-enforcement agency upon its formal written request, or pursuant to a court order.[21]

In states that have privacy laws modeled on the federal Privacy Act, state agencies are similarly restricted in disclosing medical information. Where there is no such state privacy statute, freedom-of-information or public-records laws probably exempt medical and personnel information from disclosure to the public. Such statutes would not ordinarily, however, prevent state agencies from disclosing medical information to other agencies, or even to certain private organizations, such as insurers or social-services organizations operating under contract to the state. Exempted categories under freedom-of-information acts do not enjoy any special guarantee of confidentiality; they are merely exceptions to an agency's affirmative duty to make the records available to the public.

Disclosure of medical information contained in school and college records is governed by the Family Educational Rights and Privacy Act (see Chapter II).

Information received by insurance companies has no special legal protection. Insurers freely share medical records with each other—the insurance industry's Medical Information Bureau holds medical data on 11 million insurance applicants and policyholders submitted by some 700 member U.S. and Canadian companies, from which any member company is eligible to draw information on an applicant or claimant. Insurers are legally free to give medical information to employers, to credit-reporting agencies, and to law-enforcement and other government agencies.

Credit-reporting agencies sell medical information in the normal course of their business. The Fair Credit Reporting Act permits them to sell such information to any employer, insurer, creditor, or other person having a legitimate business need as defined by the act (see Chapter IV).

Except in a handful of states, private employers are legally free to disclose medical information about current or former employees to just about anyone (see Chapter VIII).

Thus, if the third-party recipient of medical information is a governmental agency, there may be some statutory limitations—though often not very stringent—on the agency's freedom to make further disclosures. Where there is no statute, the agency's own regulations may lay down some legally enforceable restrictions. If the third-party recipient is a private organization, however, there are usually no restraints at all, except for those the organization chooses to place upon itself. Unfortunately, once medical information has left the doctor's office or the hospital record room, it is virtually unprotected by law.

Do patients have a legal right of access to their own medical records?

Frequently not. Long-established tradition and, under most circumstances, statute law and judicial decisions tend to reinforce the presumption that medical records are the property of the doctor and the hospital, not of the patient. In addition, it has long been the attitude of the medical profession that a patient cannot properly understand and interpret his own medical records, and indeed might even suffer emotional harm if allowed free access to their contents. Although there are growing numbers of dissenters within the profession, the general acceptance of this view by the medical and lay communities alike has hindered attempts to provide legally enforceable avenues of access by patients to their own records. With some notable exceptions, the courts and the legislatures have deferred to traditional wisdom on the question of patient access.

But there are encouraging signs of change. More and more practitioners, including psychiatrists, are coming around to the view that a well-informed patient is a good patient because he is equipped to take an active, cooperative part in his own care and treatment. At the same time, the growing trend of consumerism within the lay community is challenging the traditional assumption that "doctor knows best," and is recasting the relationship between doctor and patient as a working partnership in which the patient has the right to make his own informed choices and decisions, the corollary of that right being the right of access to his own records. A third factor creating a change of attitude is the public's growing realization that medical records are widely used outside the medical community to make important decisions about people's lives; that people are constantly being forced to turn their medical records over to employers, insurers, government agencies, and other third-party users without any knowledge of what those records contain. The Privacy Protection Study Commission found this, in fact, to be the most compelling argument for a right of patient access:

> Indeed, in the final analysis, the most persuasive line of reasoning favoring access [turns] on the concept of authorization. So long as it is thought acceptable, or even necessary, for an individual's past or present medical condition to be taken into account in making non-medical decisions about him, he will be asked to allow others to have access to his medical records or at least some of the information in them. As a practical matter, however, his authorization allowing such access by a third party will be meaningless so long as he does not know, and cannot find out, what is in the records. Both theoretically and practically, authorization is a meaningless procedure unless the individual knows what he is authorizing to be disclosed.[22]

What statutes give patients the right to examine and copy their own medical records?

The federal Privacy Act of 1974 provides for the individual's right to examine and copy any of his records held by federal agencies, including federal hospitals and other federal facilities. But there is a separate provision in the act dealing with access to medical records. These may be subject to "special procedures, if deemed necessary."[23] As interpreted in guidelines developed by the Office of Management and Budget, the act thus permits an indirect method of access in situations in which the agency believes that an individual might be "adversely affected" if allowed to read the full record for himself.[24] The usual "special procedures" used by agencies are to release the records to a physician or other health-care professional of the individual's choice, or to any "responsible person" designated by the individual. The person receiving the records then decides whether to turn them over to the individual.

The clumsiness of such "special procedures" is simply a legacy of the diehard attitude that there is danger in a person's knowledge of his own medical and emotional state of health. Oft-mentioned examples are the risks of a revelation of a psychiatric evaluation or terminal illness. In fact, however, few medical records seem to pose such problems. The Privacy Protection Study Commission noted the absence of any witness at the Commission's hearings who "was able to identify an instance where access to records has had an untoward effect on a patient's medical condition." [25] In practice, most federal agencies release medical records directly to the individual. The Department of Defense, for example, told the Commission that it released records to a physician rather than to the individual directly in less than 1 percent of the requests for access.[26]

Other federal privacy statutes also provide for such indirect access to medical records. The Fair Credit Reporting Act allows credit-reporting agencies to withhold medical information obtained from physicians, hospitals, and other medical personnel and facilities when it informs individuals of the "nature and substance" of their records.[27] This means, of course, that most of the information in the files of an organization like the Medical Information Bureau will be exempt from the right of access under the FCRA. Many credit-reporting agencies, including MIB, will nevertheless release medical information to a physician designated by the individual.

The Family Educational Rights and Privacy Act similarly limits students' rights to examine and copy medical and psychiatric records maintained by the institution's medical personnel. These records may be released to a physician of the student's choice. The medical records of precollege students under eighteen will be released to their parents.[28]

Nearly half the states have statutes allowing some sort of patient access to medical records, but they vary widely in their applicability to public hospitals and clinics, private hospitals, private physicians, psychiatrists, and psychiatric hospitals. Most are, in fact, quite narrowly drawn.

In Colorado, whose statute is broader than that of any other state, a patient may, for a reasonable fee, obtain copies of records kept by hospitals, private physicians, and psychiatrists (the latter only after termination of treatment).[29] In Oklahoma, a patient may examine and copy both hospital and physician records, but not psychiatric records.[30] In Massachusetts, patients may examine their hospital records both during and after their hospital stay.[31] In Mississippi, a patient wishing to obtain access to his hospital records must show "good cause," [32] but in Hawaii, a patient may have a copy of his physician or hospital records unless the health-care provider determines that the release would be detrimental to his health.[33] Oregon requires that public hospitals release records to patients within sixty days of a written request, but the disclosure may be "in the form of an accurate, representative summary," and psychiatric data may be withheld if its release "would constitute an immediate and grave detriment to the treatment of the patient." [34] Some states do not guarantee a right of access by the patient under any circumstances, but give that right to a relative or attorney.

In addition to these laws dealing specifically with access to medical records, state privacy acts modeled on the federal Privacy Act of 1974 usually provide for similar "special procedures" for the release of medical records by state agencies, state hospitals, etc.

A word of warning is in order: even in states that have some form of statutory right of access, doctors and hospitals often do not comply, and patients may have to sue to enforce the statute. The National Bureau of Standards report mentioned earlier cited two studies of the implementation of the Massachusetts act, for example: a 1973 survey showing that nine out of ten major Boston-area hospitals denied patients' requests for records, and a 1975 survey showing that only three out of twenty-eight hospitals complied.[35]

Where there is no statutory right of access, or the statute covers only certain records, how can patients get access to their medical records?

There are three possible methods.

The path of least resistance is to find a physician who will agree beforehand to obtain the records on the patient's behalf and turn them over to the patient intact. A physician's request to another practitioner or hospital for patient records is almost always honored.

The second method—certainly not to be recommended — is to file a malpractice or negligence lawsuit simply as a means for obtaining the records through a court order. This is a tremendously expensive and wasteful strategy, and a painful one for both plaintiff and defendant, but in a few instances has unfortunately been the only way open.

A third, far less drastic method is sometimes available.

In a few states, statutes or hospital-licensing regulations require physicians and hospitals to turn patient records over to the patient's attorney on demand. Even where there is no such statute or regulation, an attorney's request is often honored, though there are no guarantees. Under this procedure, the attorney presents the patient's signed and notarized authorization to the physician or hospital, obtains the records, and then, by prearrangement, turns the records over to the patient.

How have the courts ruled on questions of patient access to medical records?

There is no consistent judicial doctrine.

Over the last several decades both state and federal courts have been moving toward a broader recognition of a right of patient access, relying on at least three different lines of argument:

1. The applicability of state public-records statutes to patient records held by public hospitals.[36]
2. The legal status of the physician or hospital as the mere custodian of the record rather than its "owner," and the corollary proprietary interest of the patient in the information contained in the record.[37]
3. The patient's need for information in order to give informed consent to treatment.[38]

But the courts remain reluctant to nullify the physician's ultimate control over patient access to medical records. Several courts have permitted the withholding of certain information that would, in a physician's judgment, seriously alarm a patient to the point where he might suffer actual harm or be rendered unable to make rational judgments.[39]

Despite a number of favorable decisions in both state and federal courts, judicial recognition of the right of access is not a firmly established principle on which a patient can rely. For example, a former mental patient writing a book about her treatment was denied access to her hospital records, a denial upheld by the federal district court on the grounds that "neither the statutory, administrative, nor decisional law of New York recognizes a former patient's entitlement to his medical files in the absence of pending litigation." The court's statement that it "cannot visualize how the withholding of an indisputably confidential medical record constituted a deprivation of the plaintiff's right to privacy" is typical of the prevailing judicial refusal to recognize information privacy as a constitutional issue.[40]

May a patient correct inaccurate information in a medical record?

Yes, if the incorrect information is in a record held by a person or agency subject to a statute that provides for a right of correction. These include the federal Privacy Act and its state analogs, the Fair Credit Reporting Act, and the Family Educational Rights and Privacy Act. The correction of technical information, such as a diagnosis or the results of a laboratory test, will almost certainly require a submission by a doctor or other professional source. Thus, for example, a person who finds erroneous medical information in his Social Security Administration file will probably have to support his demand for correction, under the federal Privacy Act, with documentation prepared by a qualified professional—a procedure that will often entail more trouble and expense than are required for the correction of other kinds of data.

In practice, the patient's ability to correct medical records, or medical information in records maintained by nonmedical users, is hampered by the lack of an effective right of patient access. Naturally, a patient cannot correct a record if he cannot first read it. Although errors in doctor and hospital records can of course cause harm, the greater danger lies in errors of medical information contained in third-party records, such as those of employers, insurers, and credit-reporting agencies. Where medical information will be used to make nonmedical decisions, it is of the greatest importance for patients to utilize every avenue available to obtain access to the information and its correction or amendment. Patients should not be reluctant to challenge what the record-keepers may assert to be outside the province of the layman. As the Privacy Protection Study Commission wrote, "while it is true that some portion of the information in a medical record may be beyond the patient's comprehension, not all of it will be. . . . [T]he circulation of erroneous, obsolete, incomplete, or irrelevant medical-record information outside the confines of the medical-care relationship can bring substantial harm or embarrassment. . . ." For this reason, the Commission recommended the provision of a correction procedure applicable to all medical records and to medical information contained in all third-party nonmedical records.[41]

NOTES

1. The U.S. Supreme Court declined to review—and thus left in effect—a federal appeals court decision upholding an exception in California's privilege statute that allows a psychiatrist to be ordered to testify about a patient if the patient has himself raised the issue of his own emotional state, such as in a negligence suit. Caesar v. Mountanes, 542 F.2d 1064 (9th Cir., 1976), *cert. denied* 97 U.S. 1598 (1977).
2. FED. R. EVID. 501.
3. Whalen v. Roe, 429 U.S. 589 (1977).
4. CAL. CIV. CODE §56.
5. Womeldorf (Cox) v. Gleason, Civ. No. B–75–1086 (D.Md., Nov. 16, 1977).
6. 15 U.S.C. 1681d.
7. *See, e.g.*, the Social Security Amendments of 1972, Pub. L. No. 92–603, §249F, establishing professional-standards review organizations for the Medicare, Medicaid, and Maternal and Child Health Programs; 42 U.S.C. 4582 and 21 U.S.C. 1175, protecting the confidentiality of patient records in federally funded drug- and alcohol-abuse-treatment programs used in research projects; 42 U.S.C. 242m, governing records obtained by the National Center for Health Statistics.
8. OR. REV. STAT. §179.505.
9. 5 U.S.C. 552a.
10. 45 C.F.R. 99.31 and 99.36; 5 U.S.C. 552a(b)(8).
11. 42 C.F.R. 2.1*ff.*, authorized under 42 U.S.C. 4582 and 21 U.S.C. 1175.
12. People v. Newman, 32 N.Y.2d 379, 298 N.E.2d 651 (N.Y.Ct.App., 1973).
13. Planned Parenthood of Central Missouri v. Danforth, 428 U.S. 52 (1976).
14. *In re* Schulman v. New York City Health & Hosp. Corp., 379 N.Y.2d 702 (1975).
15. N.Y. CIV. RIGHTS LAW §79(j).
16. See, e.g., Haw. Rev. Stat. §577A–3 and 4, in which dis-

closure is mandatory for pregnancy and discretionary for V.D.

17. Horne v. Patton, 291 Ala. 701, 287 So.2d 824 (1973); Note, *Physicians and Surgeons: Civil Liability for a Physician Who Discloses Medical Information Obtained within the Doctor-Patient Relationship, in a Nonlitigation Setting,* 28 OKLA. L. REV. 3d 658–73 (1975).

18. Alan F. Westin, Computers, Health Records, and Citizen Rights (National Bureau of Standards, December 1976).

19. Principles of Medical Ethics of the American Medical Association, §9 (1957).

20. *See, e.g.,* Simenson v. Swenson, 177 S.W. 831 (Neb., 1920), a hotel doctor's disclosure to the landlord that one of the hotel guests had syphilis; Berry v. Moench, 331 P.2d 814 (Utah, 1958), a doctor's disclosure of psychiatric information about a former patient to the parents of the patient's fiancée; Clark v. Geraci, 208 N.Y.S.2d 564 (S.Ct.N.Y.,1960), a doctor's disclosure to an employer that his patient was an alcoholic; Hague v. Williams, 181 A.2d 345 (N.J.,1962), a doctor's disclosure to an insurance company of a baby's congenital heart defect that was unknown to the parents. *Note also* Tarasoff v. Regents, 529 P.2d 553 (Cal.,1974), *rehearing* 551 P.2d 334 (Cal.,1976), in which it was held that a psychiatrist has an affirmative duty to warn the intended victim of a violent patient, a decision much criticized for its implications for the right of psychiatric confidentiality.

21. 5 U.S.C. 552a(b).

22. Privacy Protection Study Commission, Personal Privacy in an Information Society 289 (U.S. Government Printing Office, July 1977).

23. 5 U.S.C. 552a(f)(3).

24. Office of Management and Budget, Privacy Act Guidelines, Vol. 40, No. 132 Fed. Reg., 28,957.

25. Privacy Protection Study Commission, *supra* note 22, at 297.

26. *Id.*

27. 15 U.S.C. 1681g(a)(1).

28. 20 U.S.C. 1232g(a)(4); 45 C.F.R. 99.3.

29. COLO. REV. STAT. §§25–1–801 and 802.

30. OKLA. STAT. ANN. tit. 76, §19.

31. MASS. ANN. LAWS ch. 111, §70.

32. MISS. CODE ANN. §7146–53.

33. HAW. REV. STAT. §622–52.

34. ORE. REV. STAT. §179.505.

35. NBS Report, *supra* note 18, at 28.

36. Morris v. Houster, 377 S.W.2d 841 (Texas Civ. App., 1964).

37. Pyramid Life Ins. Co. v. Masonic Hosp., 191 F.Supp. 51 (W.D.Ok., 1961); Emmet v. Eastern Dispensary and Cas. Hosp., 396 F.2d 931 (D.C.Cir., 1967).
38. Natanson v. Kline, 186 Kan. 393 (1960).
39. Cobbs v. Grant, 502 P.2d 1 (Cal., 1972); Natanson v. Kline, *supra* note 38.
40. Gotkin v. Miller, 379 F.Supp. 859 (1974), at 868, 864; *aff'd*, 514 F.2d 125 (1975).
41. Privacy Protection Study Commission, *supra* note 22, at 300.

VIII

Employment Records

How do employers get information about their employees, and about job applicants?

Often from the employee or applicant himself, through questionnaires, interviews, and responses to an employer's periodic queries during the person's period of employment. In addition, personality and psychological tests, polygraph tests, skills tests, and medical examinations may be performed, both before and during employment.

In considering job applicants, employers may also question former employers and professional references, ask for educational, military, credit, and medical records, and check with the police and FBI for arrest and conviction information. Some employers make these background checks themselves; others use a credit-reporting agency to do the job for them. A credit-reporting agency may also be asked to conduct an investigation on an employee who is being considered for a promotion. For certain kinds of employment requiring security clearance, a government agency will run a thorough security investigation.

While a person is employed, the employer may receive information about him from outside sources. Medical information submitted on claims under company insurance plans is usually available to at least some management personnel. Employers may be contacted by third parties with regard to a person's loan or mortgage applications, debts, suits, or garnishments. Law-enforcement and other government agencies may inform employers about the nature of their dealings with a particular employee.

Are there any restrictions on the kinds of information that employers may obtain?

As a practical matter, very few.

There are some state laws that forbid employers to ask

applicants for certain kinds of information. For example, Illinois, California, Massachusetts, and New York prohibit most employers from asking applicants about arrests not followed by a conviction. Massachusetts bars inquiries about treatment or institutionalization in a mental hospital; Michigan forbids employers to keep records describing an employee's political associations or nonemployment activities; Maryland law forbids employers to ask about psychiatric or psychological problems unless these have a direct bearing on the applicant's fitness for the particular job in question.[1]

But with a handful of exceptions such as these, employers are legally free to ask applicants just about anything, including the most intimate details of their personal lives. Employers are forbidden by state and federal laws to discriminate against applicants on the basis of certain factors—race, sex, age, handicap, religion, national origin —but not to ask the questions. (Indeed, maintaining records of the race, sex, age, etc., of both successful and unsuccessful applicants may be required in order to measure an employer's compliance with antidiscrimination laws.) Under most circumstances they may even ask applicants to reveal information that is legally confidential; a frequent item on application forms is a question about juvenile offenses, even though the records of juvenile convictions are statutorily protected and may be sealed or expunged after a person reaches his majority.

If there is any doubt about an employer's right to ask for certain types of information, applicants are routinely requested to sign waivers of confidentiality that permit the employer (or a credit-reporting agency working for him) to obtain information and records from virtually any source. Unless the applicant is in a strong bargaining position—which of course most applicants are not—he has no realistic choice but to sign the waiver. At most, it may be possible for an applicant to ask that the employer make a vaguely worded waiver more specific, for example, by indicating which sources and record-keepers he intends to query, and by inserting an expiration date.

Tipping the balance even further against the applicant's privacy are the various state and federal laws that either permit or require certain kinds of information for employment and occupational-licensing purposes. The most common focus of such laws is arrest information, even where an arrest was not followed by conviction and bears no rational relationship to the nature of the employment.

Applicants who may be tempted to protect themselves against an embarrassing or damaging disclosure by lying must remember that the disclosure may occur anyway in the course of the employer's background check or an investigation by a credit-reporting agency. Some employers view the deliberate submission of misinformation on an application as sufficient reason for refusal to hire, or even to fire an employee already on the job.

(See also Chapter IV for a discussion of preemployment investigations by credit-reporting agencies; Chapters X and XI for more on preemployment polygraph and personality tests; Chapter VII for employer access to medical information.)

Though the situation is discouraging as measured by the state of the law, a number of employers, especially large corporations, have been reappraising their application forms and procedures because of growing public concern for the right of individual privacy—and also, perhaps, as a hedge against restrictive legislation. Some of these employers have acknowledged that many items of information traditionally requested on application forms or in background investigations are not really helpful in assessing a person's qualifications or predicting his job performance. As employers become more conscious of issues of privacy, many more will undoubtedly make voluntary revisions in their collection and uses of information about both present and prospective employees. The fact remains, however, that without specific statutory protections, the applicant or employee has little leverage to resist an employer's demand for personal information.

Do employees have a right of access to their own employment records?

Most employees of government agencies have a right of access, under statute or regulation, to at least some of their employment records. Employees and former employees of federal agencies have a right of access under the Privacy Act of 1974; they are in fact the primary users of the act's access provisions.[2] In states that have analogous privacy acts, employees of state and local agencies have similar statutory access rights. State freedom-of-information laws often can be used by government employees to obtain access to their own employment records. Access provisions are commonly contained in state civil-service regulations. All of these laws and regulations differ in their designations of certain kinds of records that employees may not see; frequent exceptions are medical records, performance evaluations, test results, and security and investigatory files.

In the private sector, however, employees have statutory rights of access to their employment records in only a few states.[3] In California, for example, an employer must by law permit the employee to examine his records, at reasonable times on request, but may withhold letters of reference and certain other documents. In Maine, such references are open to inspection by both present and former employees. In Oregon, present employees may inspect records that have been used as the basis for hiring, promotion, disciplinary action, and termination, and former employees may obtain a certified copy of their records within sixty days of leaving their jobs.

In the states that have no access statutes for private employees, some employees may have rights of access under union contracts, or by the voluntarily adopted policies of their employers. A number of large corporations have experimented with open-records policies in recent years. These usually contain certain exceptions, often for such categories of records as security files, medical records (sometimes made available to the employee's physician rather than to the employee directly), psychological-test results, information supplied by confidential sources, and, frequently, performance evaluations, supervisors' opinions, disciplinary reports, and promotion recommendations.

As a general rule, therefore, a public employee may assume that he has a legally enforceable right of access under an applicable federal or state statute or civil-service regulation to at least some of his employment records; a private employee must assume that he has no legally enforceable right unless he lives in one of the very few states that has legislated such a right. Even without statutory guarantees, however, employees should press their employers and supervisors to grant them access to, at the very least, those records that could be used to make decisions affecting the conditions of their employment or be revealed to outside parties. The obvious logic of the arguments for access to such records seems to be leading increasing numbers of employers to reevaluate their traditionally secretive policies.

Do employees have a right to correct or amend their records?

Public employees whose records are covered by federal and state privacy acts have the right to ask that inaccurate, incomplete, irrelevant, or outdated data be corrected, and to place statements of disagreement in their files if the record is not corrected. In a few states, rights of amendment are provided under statutes pertaining specifically to employee records.[4] Civil-service regulations in some states provide limited opportunities to amend personnel records. Some private employers have voluntarily instituted policies allowing employees to challenge the accuracy of the contents of their files and even, in some cases, the subjective performance evaluations written by their supervisors. But these opportunities are provided solely at the employer's discretion; they are not enforceable under law.

Are employment records confidential under law?

If the employer is a federal agency, the Privacy Act of 1974 defines the confidentiality of employment records. The act permits disclosures of federal-agency employee records without the employee's consent only for "routine uses," in response to the written request of a law-enforcement agency, or in compliance with a court order. In states with analogous privacy acts, employment records held by state and local agencies may enjoy similar protections. A few states have special statutes protecting the confidentiality of state employees' records.[5] Civil-service regulations in some other states may provide limited protections for confidentiality.

But if the employer is a private business or corporation, there are no comprehensive statutory protections for the confidentiality of employment records.[6] Occasionally, union contracts provide some protections. Otherwise, the matter lies solely in the discretion of the employer. To understand just how crucial the exercise of that discretion really is, one must recall that employment files ordinarily contain much more than strictly job-related information; they may have medical, family, sexual, financial, political, and other personal data, and often also the subjective comments of colleagues and supervisors. The confidentiality of all this lies completely at the employer's mercy.

Does this mean that there is no legal recourse for a person whose employer has given out information about him without his permission?

Not entirely. In some very special circumstances there may be redress.

If the information is false and defamatory, and if it is directly responsible for causing a serious tangible injury to the employee, there may be grounds for recovery of damages in a defamation lawsuit. But a provable combination of such conditions is rare.

Employers routinely disclose information about their employees to other employers, unions, law-enforcement agencies and various other government agencies, banks and creditors, insurance companies, and private individuals. Some of these disclosures may be legally mandated or in compliance with the employee's own wishes; others may be offensive to his sense of privacy, or even cause him actual harm. Although most of the information disclosed by employers is job-related, some disclosures may reveal aspects of the employee's personal life, such as his sexual orientation, political associations, or family problems. Yet, unless the circumstances are unusual, the private employer cannot be legally penalized for violating the employee's privacy.

Where the employer is a government agency subject to the federal Privacy Act or an analogous state statute, an aggrieved employee can bring a lawsuit for disclosures made in violation of those statutes. Under the federal Privacy Act, for example, a person who suffers an "adverse effect" because of a "willful and intentional" disclosure of records made in violation of the act can sue for damages of at least $1000, and an official who "knowingly and willfully" makes such a disclosure can be fined up to $5000.[7]

But for most private employees, there is no legally established "expectation of confidentiality" in their employment records. Unless a disclosure rises to the level of an actual defamation (a matter on which an attorney's advice should be sought), there is no readily available remedy, however offensive or prejudicial the disclosure may be.

Is there any legal recourse for a person whose former employer gives a damaging reference to a prospective employer?

Not much, unless the reference actually contains false and defamatory statements.

People sometimes attribute their inability to obtain employment to damaging statements made by a former employer. Assuming that a person is able to get access to the references in his employment files, a lawsuit for defamation may be possible. Oral statements present a greater problem, since there is unlikely to be any documentary evidence or third-party witness. The situation is more favorable when the reference is delivered to the prospective employer by a credit-reporting agency, for here the person is entitled, under the Fair Credit Reporting Act, to learn at least the "nature and substance" of the information in the agency's files.

Having discovered the nature of the former employer's reference, and having determined, on an attorney's advice, that a defamation suit is not a practical option, the employee can only attempt to combat the effects of the derogatory reference by giving his own explanation and interpretation to prospective employers, and perhaps by presenting testimonials from other employers, supervisors, and coworkers.

If the advantages seem to be stacked heavily in the employer's favor, it should be noted that employers seem to be increasingly deterred by the threat of defamation suits—which are a nuisance and an expense to defend even if the plaintiff eventually loses—and therefore increasingly loath to give wholly unflattering references. In fact, employers sometimes claim that they hesitate to give even clearly truthful derogatory references for fear of lawsuits. While that claim is probably overstated, more and more employers are taking steps to make provision for employees to examine—and in some cases comment upon and rebut—the performance evaluations that go into their files and that could be disclosed in references to future employers.

NOTES

1. *See* ILL. REV. STAT. ch. 48, §853(e); CAL. LAB. CODE §432.7; MASS. ANN. LAWS ch. 276, §§100A and C, and ch. 151B, §4; N.Y. CORREC. LAW §§750 *et seq.*; MICH. COMP. LAWS ANN. §§423.501 *et seq.*; MD. ANN. CODE art. 100, §95A.

2. *See, e.g.,* FEDERAL PERSONAL DATA SYSTEMS SUBJECT TO THE PRIVACY ACT OF 1974, Second Annual Report of the President, Calendar Year 1976 (Government Printing Office, 1977), and subsequent Annual Reports.

3. *See* CAL. LAB. CODE §1198.5; OR. REV. STAT. §652.750; MICH. COMP. LAWS ANN. *supra* note 1; ME. REV. STAT. tit. 26, §631; PA. STAT. ANN. tit. 43 §§1321 *et seq.* Connecticut's Public Act 79–264 is effective January 1, 1981.

4. *See, e.g.,* N.C. GEN. STAT. §§126–24 *et seq.* (public employees); MICH. COMP. LAWS ANN., *supra* note 1 (private employees).

5. *See, e.g.,* COLO. REV. STAT., §24–50–127; N.C. GEN. STAT., *supra* note 4.

6. There are minor exceptions to this generalization; for example, the Michigan Employee Right-to-Know Act (*supra* note 1) places some restrictions on the kinds of information —particularly adverse information—that an employer may disclose.

7. 5 U.S.C. 552a(g) and (i).

IX

Social Security Numbers

Is the Social Security number a universal identifier?

Not technically, but the Social Security number (SSN) is so widely used as an identifier by both government and private agencies that many people consider it to be a *de facto* universal identifier nonetheless.

To be a true universal identifier, a label would have to be unique to each person: no more than one person would have a given number, and no person would have more than one number. A person would carry the same number throughout his life, and it would not be reused after his death. It would contain internal check features so that errors in transcription or communication could be detected easily.

The SSN does not meet these criteria. Many people have more than one number. Some numbers have been issued to or used by more than one person. The SSN does not contain any internal check features, and it can easily be deliberately falsified or inadvertently misreported.[1]

But these technical deficiencies have not prevented such widespread reliance on the SSN for authentication and identification purposes that the number is popularly accepted and treated as a universal identifier, and so it must be regarded as such.

Why is a universal identifier a threat to the right of privacy?

The use of a common label to identify the records of individuals in many separate record systems makes it easier, cheaper, and therefore more practical to exchange, compare, and combine information among those various systems. This in turn makes it easier for government agencies and private organizations to trace any individual virtually from cradle to grave, and thus encloses each person ever more tightly in a "record prison," unable to escape his past or protect any aspect of his life from scrutiny. It must be emphasized that the absence of a universal identifier will not by itself prevent the pooling and linking of records, particularly with today's sophisticated computer technology, nor does the use of a universal identifier by itself cause record linking. The availability of a universal identifier simply makes such linking easier, and therefore more likely to occur. An example of a particularly wide-ranging record-linking project through use of the SSN is the comparison of employment, unemployment compensation, Social Security, and welfare records under Project Match, described in Chapter VI.

Another danger of the universal identifier is that it gives impetus to the development of a mandatory national identity document. If each person has a single number that can be used to identify and authenticate all of his records, an identity card would be a handy means of establishing not only his identity but also his entitlement to certain benefits and privileges. A familiar example is the recurring proposal for an identity card to be carried by all citizens and resident aliens who are legally entitled to hold a job in the United States, a device intended to discourage the employment of undocumented ("illegal") aliens. The confiscation, or even the threat of confiscation, of such a document would be a formidable means of controlling people's behavior. The demand to "show one's papers" has long been regarded as the hallmark of a police state.

A third danger is the likelihood that a national population register would probably become necessary to authenticate the universal identifier. To prevent forgery, fraud, and bureaucratic error, the information on an identity card would have to be verifiable through comparison with a population register. Such a register could easily become the basis for a national databank—the much-feared "one big dossier" compiled and maintained on each individual from birth to death.

What kinds of record systems use the SSN as an identifier?

The original use of the SSN, of course, was to number personal accounts for the collection of taxes and payment of benefits in the Social Security program. The first numbers were assigned in 1936. A year later, it was decided that the same identifier should be used to number accounts in state unemployment-insurance systems. In 1943, Executive Order 9397 was issued, authorizing any federal agency to use the SSN for new data systems requiring permanent account numbers on records pertaining to individuals, although this authority was not used for many years, even by the federal Civil Service Commission, for whose benefit it was originally intended.

In 1961 the Internal Revenue Service decided to designate the SSN as the taxpayer identification number. Thereafter, new uses by government agencies followed in rapid succession: for Treasury bonds, for old-age-assistance benefits accounts, for state and federal civil-service employee records, for Veterans' Administration hospital records, for Indian Health Service patient records, as the military-personnel service number, for customer records in bank and securities transactions, for motor-vehicle registration and driver's licenses in many states, and for client records (including those of children) in local, state, and federal public-assistance programs. In almost every personal-data system maintained by a federal, state, or local agency, the SSN is now the identifier.

In private data systems, the SSN is frequently used for such purposes as insurance policies, department-store charge accounts and credit-card accounts, telephone- and utility-company accounts, patient records, student identification numbers, library cards, and membership records in labor unions and professional associations.

What laws require a person to disclose his SSN to, or allow its use by, a government agency?

As just noted, many federal, state, and local agencies adopted regulations requiring use of the SSN for their personal-data systems in the four decades following the enactment of Social Security. The Privacy Act of 1974, however, placed a moratorium on new uses of the SSN by government agencies as of January 1, 1975. Unless a government agency, pursuant to statute or a formally adopted regulation, had the authority to use the SSN for identification purposes in specific record systems before that date, it could not establish new uses except by explicit Congressional authorization.[2]

Since the passage of the Privacy Act, Congress has established several new permissible governmental uses. Under the Tax Reform Act of 1976, Congress granted the states permission to use the SSN for motor-vehicle registration records and driver's licenses, for the administration of local and state tax laws, for the administration of general public-assistance (welfare) programs, and for implementation of the Parent Locator Service.[3]

The Privacy Act requires that when a government agency asks a person for his SSN, it must state its legal authority by statute or regulation for obtaining the number, whether disclosure is mandatory or voluntary, and how the number will be used.

A few states have laws restricting state and local governmental uses of the SSN.[4] In practice, these add little to the restrictions of the federal statute.

What laws require a person to disclose his SSN to a private business or agency?

None.

Private organizations have no specific legal authority to use or demand the disclosure of the SSN, except insofar as they must do so to satisfy government requirements. An employer, for example, must by law obtain his employees' SSNs for tax and Social Security purposes, but there is no statute allowing him to use it as a general employee identifier for all personnel records.

On the other hand, neither are private organizations legally prevented from using or demanding the disclosure of the SSN. If a person refuses to give his number, there is no law to prevent a private organization from refusing to do business with him. For practical purposes, therefore, private organizations are free to use the SSN to the extent that their customers and clients acquiesce.

What should a person do when presented with a demand for his SSN?

If the demand comes from a government agency, the person should not comply until the agency meets its obligations under the Privacy Act of 1974 to (1) cite its formal legal authority for using the number, (2) reveal whether disclosure is mandatory or voluntary, (3) explain how the number will be used. Unless the number will be used for records of taxes, motor-vehicle registration, driver's licenses, or general public assistance, or for implementation of the Parent Locator System, the agency's legal authority to use the number must predate January 1, 1975.[5]

If the demand comes from a private agency or business and is not required for governmental purposes, the individual should stand his ground as long as possible, and if he cares enough, take his business elsewhere. That, of course, may not be so easy, as more and more private organizations are using the SSN for their own record systems.

Will the courts support a person's refusal to disclose his SSN?

In some circumstances.

Before the enactment of the Privacy Act, few courts listened sympathetically to arguments that the use of the SSN by government agencies was a threat to the constitutional right of privacy.[6] Since passage of the act, judicial tests of SSN uses have focused primarily on statutory rather than constitutional interpretation: that is, whether a particular use is or is not authorized by the Privacy Act as amended by the Tax Reform Act of 1976. Several lawsuits have been filed to challenge the assignment and disclosure of SSNs for the minor children of welfare recipients. At least one court ruled that where statute law does not explicitly require the enumeration of minor children for a particular welfare program, the administering agency may not do so by regulation, but the question remains at issue in other jurisdictions and for other programs.[7]

In unusual circumstances, the courts may be willing to entertain constitutional as well as statutory analysis. A federal district court in New York upheld the refusal of a family of welfare recipients to obtain SSNs for their children, accepting the parents' assertions of their "sincerely held" religious belief that the enumeration is a "mark of the Beast" and "device of the Antichrist" forbidden by the Book of Revelation. The court in this case deferred to the plaintiffs' objections on First Amendment grounds of religious freedom, and did not venture into broader questions of the constitutional right of privacy of welfare recipients as a class.[8]

There have also been some successful instances of resistance to demands for SSNs where litigation was threatened or filed but not concluded. In response to persistent pressure by ACLU affiliates, the California Bar Association, for example, dropped its requirement for the submission of an SSN by a candidate for admission, the number was removed from fishing licenses in Maine, and several state university systems ended their requirements that SSNs be submitted by students.

In general, the person who wishes to challange what appears to be an improper use of the SSN by a public agency should not expect the courts to do more than examine existing state and federal statutes to determine whether they are being properly applied in the given circumstances. At present, it does not seem likely that the courts will question the judgment of the legislatures on the SSN, or explore the constitutional principles raised by the use of a universal identifier.

NOTES

1. For other attributes of a standard identifier and the failure of the SSN to meet those requirements, *see* SECRETARY'S ADVISORY COMMITTEE ON AUTOMATED PERSONAL DATA SYSTEMS, U.S. DEPARTMENT OF HEALTH, EDUCATION, AND WELFARE, RECORDS, COMPUTERS AND THE RIGHTS OF CITIZENS, Chapter VII (July 1973).
2. Pub. L. No. 93–579, §7.
3. Pub. L. No. 94–455, §1211.
4. *See, e.g.*, ARK. STAT. ANN. §16–801 *et seq;* OKLA. STAT. ANN. tit. 74, §3111; VA. CODE §§2.1–377 *et seq.* and §58–46.3.
5. Pub. L. No. 93–579, §7.
6. *See, e.g.*, Meyer v. Putnam, 73–1908–1 (Dist. Ct., Cty. of Boulder, 1973).
7. Green v. Philbrook, 427 F.Supp. 834 (D.Vt., 1977); *but see also* Chambers v. Klein, 419 F.Supp. 569 (D.N.J., 1976), for the opposite result.
8. Stevens v. Berger, 428 F.Supp. 896 (E.D.N.Y., 1977).

PART TWO

Intrusion into Personal Thoughts

X

Polygraphs and Psychological Stress Evaluators

What is a polygraph?

A polygraph is an instrument—really a collection of instruments—that measures changes in a person's rate of respiration, his blood pressure, and the electrical conductivity of his skin. It consists of a blood-pressure cuff strapped to the arm, tubing wrapped around the chest, and electrodes attached to the hand, all connected to pens that register physiological changes during an interview between the polygraph examiner and the test subject. Popularly known as a "lie detector," the polygraph works on the theory that the act of lying causes psychological conflict, conflict causes fear, and fear brings about certain measurable physiological changes, which are detected and recorded by the polygraph machine.

What is a psychological-stress evaluator?

The psychological-stress evaluator, or PSE, is a mechanism that measures fluctuations in the sound waves produced by the voice. It, too, works on the theory that the psychological stress produced by lying is expressed in detectable physical changes in the body that can be recorded on a machine. Similar to the PSE in function is the voice-stress analyzer. Unlike the polygraph, the PSE and voice-stress analyzer are not attached to the test subject's body. They can be hidden from sight during an interview, or used over the telephone or with a tape-recorded voice. Therefore, a "lie-detector" test using the PSE or voice-stress analyzer can be conducted completely without the knowledge of the test subject.

Can polygraphs and psychological-stress evaluators really detect lies?

Apparently not. Studies of the accuracy, reliability, and validity of "lie detectors" under controlled conditions (that is, where there is independent verification of the test subject's truthfulness) are, at best, inconclusive. The results reported in research conducted by polygraphers themselves, not surprisingly, have always been much more favorable than the results reported in independent research. Two Congressional committees that reviewed the available evidence have declared themselves unconvinced of the test's accuracy, reliability, or validity.[1]

The major weakness in claims made for the polygraph and PSE is the assumption that the physiological reactions they measure are *necessarily* caused by fear, which is itself *necessarily* caused by lying. The same physiological reactions could well be caused by other factors, such as fatigue, illness, a headache, or even the race or sex of the subject. Similarly, stress could be caused by the tension of the interview itself, by embarrassment or anger at the test questions, or by the extraneous thoughts and feelings of the subject. On the other hand, the pathological liar who feels no guilt or fear at lying, or the person who answers a question falsely but believes it to be true, will not register the expected physiological changes that are supposedly characteristic of a liar.

A second weakness is that the "detection" of lies is a function not of the machine, but of the test examiner. Both the questions and the subject's reactions are filtered through the biases, preconceptions, and attitudes of the examiner. Most examiners have little training beyond the mechanics of their machines, and virtually none in medicine or psychology. Ultimately, the results of a polygraph or PSE test are determined by the personal judgment of the examiner, just as the results of an interview without the benefit of a machine would be determined by the personal judgment of the interviewer. The only real difference is that the use of a supposedly scientific method tends to make both the examiner and the test subject give greater credence to the whole procedure.

Why are "lie-detector" tests an invasion of privacy?

First, because the attempt to reach into a person's mind and to capture his unarticulated thoughts, feelings, and motivations is by definition an invasion of privacy and a violation of human dignity. Also, the attempt to get a person to admit to cheating or committing a crime, the object of many "lie-detector" tests, is a violation of the Fifth Amendment privilege against self-incrimination and of the Fourth Amendment protection against unreasonable searches.

Second, many "lie-detector" tests, particularly those used for preemployment screening, delve into areas that ought to be beyond inquiry: mental illnesses, use of drugs and alcohol, marital problems, gambling, sexual preference, religious and political beliefs, arrests, juvenile offenses, undetected crimes, or knowledge of crimes by other employees. The atmosphere of the test creates, on the subject's part, an inducement to "confess," by convincing him that the machine will discover not only his actual spoken lies but also his attempts to evade or withhold the truth. The examiner, for his part, is led to ask ever more probing questions in order to clarify the meaning of the subject's reactions. Between the examiner's pressing and the test subject's eagerness to be deemed truthful, many intimate details of the subject's life, thoughts, and feelings can be elicited.

A third invasion of privacy results from the use of a psychological-stress evaluator or voice-stress analyzer without the subject's knowledge. Whether hidden from view or used over a telephone or with a tape-recorded conversation, these devices capture the unguarded words of a subject who is not even aware that he is being tested.

How are "lie-detector" tests used?

Their primary use is for preemployment screening. Also common is the testing of employees after the discovery of a theft or inventory shortage, and in some companies, routine periodic testing of employees "to keep them honest." An employer may ask new employees to sign a statement that they will submit to a "lie-detector" test at any time during the course of their employment at the employer's request.

The police sometimes use "lie-detector" tests to interrogate suspects, witnesses, and even victims in criminal investigations. Tests are occasionally given to parties in civil litigation, including divorce cases.

May an employer force a job applicant or employee to take a "lie-detector" test?

Yes, except in states that have statutes forbidding or restricting the use of such tests for employment purposes.

About 20 states and localities have laws that prohibit "lie-detector" tests as a precondition of employment.[2] Many of them, however, permit an employer to "request" or "suggest" that an applicant submit to "voluntary" testing, and nearly all exempt applicants either for police employment or for any public employment. Violations are misdemeanors, punishable in most instances by a modest fine, and the laws are widely ignored by employers and infrequently enforced by prosecutors. Only in one state, New Jersey, has litigation successfully produced a meaningful civil remedy for an employee whose rights were violated under an antipolygraph statute—that is, substantial money damages and the expungement of derogatory records resulting from an illegally administered test.[3] Because the statutes provide only for criminal prosecutions of offending employers, victims of statutory violations are ordinarily left without any material restitution for the losses or damages they have suffered.

An applicant or employee in a state that has legislated restrictions on polygraph tests should certainly report employers' violations to a state prosecutor. In states without such laws, a person who resists an employer's demand that he take a test must be prepared to risk the loss of a job or job opportunity. Because the courts have not dealt with the constitutional questions raised by the use of "lie detectors" for employment purposes, resort to litigation has been unsuccessful except where rights are first established by statute. That is why privacy advocates favor a federal statutory ban on all uses of "lie detectors" in employment.

May an employer dismiss an employee who refuses to take a "lie-detector" test?

It is possible under some circumstances.

A few of the state statutes restricting polygraph tests

protect employees as well as applicants. Even so, "voluntary" submission to a test at an employer's "request" may still be allowed. Employees are naturally under enormous pressure to prove their innocence where there has been a theft or other crime against the employer, and a refusal to be tested under these circumstances is easily twisted into cause for dismissal. Where an employee's union is willing to contest such a dismissal under ordinary grievance procedures, there is some hope: the union contract may contain a protective provision, and labor-arbitration rulings have almost always overturned suspensions or dismissals based solely upon the results of a "lie-detector" test or the employee's refusal to take a test.[4]

Employees who are fired for refusing to take a test, and who do not have the protection of a union contract or recourse to arbitration, may experience difficulties in collecting unemployment-insurance benefits. In one such instance, it was ruled that a person fired for this reason was not guilty of "misconduct" and therefore not disqualified from receiving benefits, even though he had agreed to submit to testing at any time as a condition of employment.[5] Unfortunately, this interpretation is not universally held.

May the police force a person to take a "lie-detector" test?

No.

Under no circumstances should any suspect or witness agree to take a test without the advice of a lawyer. Before submitting to a test in the course of a police investigation, the person must be fully apprised of all the risks, including the chance that the results might be introduced in court. (Although test results are usually inadmissible as evidence in a criminal trial, except where both prosecution and defense agree before trial to submit a test in evidence, there have been a few exceptions.[6]) The same warning applies to parties engaged in civil litigation.

NOTES

1. SUBCOMMITTEE ON CONSTITUTIONAL RIGHTS, SENATE JUDICIARY COMMITTEE, PRIVACY, POLYGRAPHS, AND EMPLOYMENT

(November 1974); HOUSE COMMITTEE ON GOVERNMENT OPERATIONS, THE USE OF POLYGRAPHS AND SIMILAR DEVICES BY FEDERAL AGENCIES (January 1976).

2. *See* ALASKA STAT. §23.10.037; CAL. LAB. CODE, §432.2; CONN. GEN. STAT. ANN. §31–51g; DEL. CODE ANN. tit. 19, §704; HAW. REV. STAT. §378–21; IDAHO CODE, §§44,903–904; MD. ANN. CODE art.100, §95; MASS. ANN. LAWS ch. 149, §19–B; MICH. COMP. LAWS ANN. §§338.1701 *et seq.;* MINN. STAT. ANN. §181.75; MONT. REV. CODES ANN. §§41.119–120; N.J. STAT. ANN. §2A:170–90.1; OR. REV. STAT. §§659.225 and 703; PA. STAT. ANN. tit. 18, §7321; R.I. GEN. LAWS §§28–6.1–1 and 2; WASH. REV. CODE ANN. §49.44.120 N.Y. LAB. LAW §733 prohibits preemployment use of the PSE. Several cities have enacted restrictive ordinances against polygraphs. A few states that license polygraphers provide penalties for queries into certain aspects of the test subject's life.

3. Humphrey v. First Nat'l State Bank, Civ. Action No. 76–24 (D.N.J., 1977).

4. PRIVACY, POLYGRAPHS, AND EMPLOYMENT, *supra* note 1, at 15 n. 100; *see also* Amalgamated Jewelry, Diamond and Watchcase Workers Union v. Art Carved, Inc., American Arbitration Assn. Case No. 1330–0848–77 (New York, Nov. 14, 1977).

5. Appeal Board, Unemployment Insurance Division, New York State Department of Labor, No. 226,217, Sept. 8, 1976.

6. PRIVACY, POLYGRAPHS, AND EMPLOYMENT, *supra* note 1, at 14–15.

XI

Psychological Testing and Questionnaires

Are preemployment psychological, personality, and "character" tests an invasion of privacy?

Many privacy advocates believe that they are. Standardized tests and questionnaires that attempt to measure an applicant's character, opinions, attitudes, propensities, and emotional make-up frequently delve into areas of personal thought and feeling that ought to be protected against uninvited intrusions by employers or any other outsider. This is quite apart from the question of the predictive validity of preemployment psychological tests—that is, whether the psychological profile of the applicant that is constructed by the test has any value in predicting the applicant's success or failure in a particular job. Many employers who use such tests may believe that an apparently "scientific" method of screening applicants is superior to their own intuitive judgment of human character, but this has never been definitely proved.

Some tests may be directly relevant to a specific type of employment. An employer is perfectly justified in testing an applicant's capabilities in mathematical reasoning if such capabilities would be required to do a particular job. In certain circumstances, even an "attitude" test might be reasonable—for example, in determining a prospective social worker's approach to a variety of difficult situations he would encounter on the job.

But most preemployment psychological tests in common use today are not so carefully drawn. Many purport to measure personality "types" (submissive, independent, authoritarian, rebellious), predict an applicant's propensity for dishonest or criminal behavior, or reveal hidden psychological problems (social maladjustments, drug or alcohol abuse, anxieties, sexual problems). These are the kinds of tests that pose serious questions of personal privacy.

Is it legal to require preemployment psychological tests?

Yes, under present statutory and judicial law.

The Supreme Court has ruled that tests given to employment applicants that result in discrimination on grounds of race or sex must be reasonably job-related.[1] Under this standard, it might be possible to challenge some preemployment tests as insufficiently related to the requirements of a particular kind of employment, if these tests have such a discriminatory result. So far, no preemployment psychological tests have been judicially invalidated on these grounds.

An important challenge to preemployment psychological testing, on different grounds, is now in the courts. It concerns tests given to applicants to a fire department, covering such subjects as religious practice and belief, sexual preference and fantasies, reading habits, family relationships, attitudes toward crime, dishonesty, poverty, and politics, and feelings of depression, rejection, and fear.[2] The plaintiffs are hoping to show that such testing violates applicants' constitutional freedoms of belief and speech and constitutional right of privacy.

Is psychological testing of schoolchildren an invasion of privacy?

It is difficult to generalize, because children are subjected to so many different kinds of intelligence, aptitude, achievement, diagnostic, attitude, and personality tests over the course of their years in school.

Where tests are given to measure a child's intellectual capabilities or knowledge of subject matter, questions of privacy do not ordinarily arise. Tests designed to diagnose learning, social, or emotional problems that could lead to placement in special classes or counseling programs are more likely to pose a danger to a child's right of privacy. The tests themselves as well as their uses may discriminate against certain groups of children on the basis of race or ethnic background—as the courts have sometimes ruled on tests indicating placement in "special" or "remedial" classes [3]—or may unfairly stigmatize children by labeling them as socially or psychologically disturbed. The latter point was the finding in a 1973 federal district court decision invalidating, on constitutional privacy grounds, a questionnaire for eighth-graders designed to identify potential drug abusers by eliciting information about their thoughts, feelings, and family and social relationships.[4] In addition to the intrusiveness of the questionnaire itself, the court was disturbed by the wide circulation of the results to school personnel, social workers, school-board members, and even PTA officers, and by the lack of immunity from subpoena by law-enforcement officials.

A third and increasingly popular type of psychological testing is intended to measure children's attitudes about public affairs or human relationships. Where the test papers are not individually identified and are used only for statistical compilations, or where they remain within the classroom as a basis for discussion of social issues and attitudes, such testing programs are frequently defended for their educational utility. There are those, however, who feel that any attempt to elicit children's private feelings within the essentially coercive environment of the school is an invasion of privacy, and that testing of this sort inevitably creates norms of behavior and attitude against which children will be measured as "normal" or "deviant." These questions have not been addressed by the courts or by the legislatures.

How can schoolchildren be protected against intrusive psychological testing?

Primarily through watchfulness by parents.

Parents should make sure that their children are not given any psychological, personality, or diagnostic tests without their prior informed consent. They should not give that consent until they have received a clear explanation of the content and purpose of the test, the proposed uses of the results, and the identities of those who will have access to the results. They should also use their statutory right of access to student records (see Chapter II) to examine the results for themselves.

NOTES

1. Griggs v. Duke Power Company, 401 U.S. 424 (1971).
2. McKenna v. Fargo, *reversed and remanded*, 510 F.2d. 1179 (3rd Cir., 1975).
3. *See* ALAN LEVINE and EVE CARY, THE RIGHTS OF STUDENTS 89–95 (Avon, rev. ed., 1977).
4. Merriken v. Cressman, 364 F.Supp. 913 (E.D. Pa., 1973).

PART THREE

Collection and Control of Government Information

XII

Information Practices

How does the federal government collect information?
The federal government collects enormous quantities of information in every conceivable manner, ranging from information compiled by force of law to information procured in violation of law. At latest count, made by the Office of Management and Budget, the federal government alone maintains 5800 personal-data systems and 3.65 billion records about individuals.[1]

The law requires people to submit extensive information to the federal government. Tax information and census information are the most common, affecting virtually every adult in the country. In addition, people must submit personal information in connection with military and civilian employment, health, education and welfare programs, security clearance, passport applications, agricultural programs, etc.

Federal law-enforcement agencies actively collect arrest, conviction, and sentence data as well as intelligence dossiers which describe the subjects' political activities, personal lifestyles, habits, and judgments (or malicious gossip) of neighbors and acquaintances. Occasionally, intelligence agents open mail, eavesdrop and steal information in violation of the Constitution and criminal statutory law.

The federal government also collects information which is *voluntarily* submitted without any legal requirement. For example, a person who calls a government agency for assistance must describe the details of the problem, which are usually recorded and filed. Similarly, when people complain about the performance of a federal employee, the functioning of a particular program, or the operation of government in general, the information becomes part of the government's records.

Businesses are also the subject of a host of laws requiring the submission of voluminous and detailed information to the Internal Revenue Service, the Census Bureau, the Securities and Exchange Commission and other regulatory agencies. Even local and state governments must provide detailed information to the federal government, often containing data on individuals, in order to take advantage of federal assistance programs.

What is a dossier?

A dossier is a file containing information about a person. However, referring to a file as a "dossier" often suggests that such a file is being maintained for intelligence purposes.

The existence of these intelligence dossiers is now well documented. As of 1976 the FBI maintained 500,000 domestic-intelligence files. Between 1953 and 1973, the CIA opened 250,000 first-class letters and used the information it discovered to produce a computerized index of more than a million names. And the CIA's operation CHAOS, which continued for six years, resulted in files on 300,000 people. Similarly, other federal agencies such as the IRS, the National Security Agency, and the military intelligence units, all accumulate dossiers as a consequence of their own intelligence operations.[2]

Are there any limitations on the government's data-collection and information practices?

Yes. The Privacy Act regulates the procedures by which the government may collect, maintain, and disseminate personal information. It requires that the government abide by certain fair-information practices. In addition, the Constitution and laws of the United States contain many requirements, limitations, and restrictions which both directly and indirectly affect the way the government collects and maintains records.

The Privacy Act [3] "information practices" provisions apply to any federal executive agency, independent regulatory agency, or private contractor that operates a system of records for an agency to accomplish an agency function.[4] The Privacy Act does not govern the records maintained by legislative or judicial agencies and the information-practices provisions pertain only to information that an agency maintains in a system of records. "Maintains" is broadly defined to include maintain, collect, use, or disseminate. A "system of records" means a group of items or data about an individual from which information is retrieved by reference to the name or identifying symbol of the individual.[5] Thus a file that is maintained alphabetically according to the subject's last name, or numerically according to the subject's Social Security number, is a system of records.

In addition, the Constitution imposes some limits on data collection. For example, the Fourth Amendment protects a person's home, papers, and effects from unreasonable search and seizure. Therefore, except in certain emergencies the police cannot break into a home and take a person's diary, for example. Although the Fourth Amendment protects against extreme abuses, the Supreme Court has not interpreted the Constitution broadly to effectively limit the government's power to collect personal information. For example, the Court has ruled that New York could require pharmacists to send copies of all prescriptions for certain drugs for centralized computerization.[6]

Are there any exceptions to the information-practices provisions of the Privacy Act?

Yes. The Privacy Act contains many exceptions excluding agency records from its protections and limitations. There are two categories—general exemptions and specific exemptions.

The general exemptions[7] pertain to record systems maintained by the CIA and to record systems of law-enforcement agencies, if the record system contains (a) information compiled to identify criminal offenders, (b) information compiled for criminal investigation, or (c) any report identifiable to an individual which is compiled at any stage of the criminal-justice process.

The agencies that maintain "general-exemption records" are authorized, but not required, to promulgate regulations exempting the applicable record systems from certain of the information-practices provisions of the Privacy Act. Thus the Privacy Act allows the agencies to decide for themselves which records should be exempt. The legislative history indicates that Congress intended "to urge [the general-exemption agencies] to keep open whatever files are presently open and to make available in the future whatever files can be made available without clearly infringing on the ability of the agencies to fulfill their missions." [8] An agency's regulations are available in the *Federal Register* and will usually be sent to you by the agency upon request.

The specific exemptions [9] authorize *any* agency to exempt a system of records from certain of the information-practices provisions of the Privacy Act, but only if the system of records is:

1. subject to FOIA exemption 1 (that is, information which has been properly classified pursuant to an Executive Order);
2. investigatory material compiled for law-enforcement purposes; however, if an individual is denied any right or benefit as a result of the maintenance of this record, such record shall be provided to the individual except to the extent that disclosure would reveal the identity of a confidential source;
3. maintained in connection with providing protective services to the President;
4. required by statute to be maintained and used solely for statistical purposes;
5. investigatory material compiled solely for determining eligibility for federal civilian employment to the extent the disclosure would reveal the identity of a confidential source;
6. certain testing or examination material;
7. certain evaluation material used to determine potential for promotion in the armed forces.

Just as general-exemption records are exempted from only certain limited provisions of the Privacy Act, the specific exemption records are similarly excluded from only a few of the information-practices provisions of the Privacy Act. As with the general exemption, the agency must promulgate implementing regulations, available in the *Federal Register* or from the agencies. Again, Congress urged the agencies "to open [specific-exemption records] to the individuals named in them insofar as such action would not impair the proper functioning of the agencies." [10]

Does the Privacy Act require the government to identify its systems of records?

Yes. The government is prohibited from maintaining secret repositories of information which cannot be monitored or controlled. Therefore, the Privacy Act requires each agency which maintains a system of records to publish annually in the *Federal Register* a notice of the existence and character of the system,[11] including:

1. the name and location of the system;
2. the categories of individuals on whom records are maintained in the system;
3. the categories of records maintained in the system;
4. each routine use of the records contained in the system, including the categories of users and the purpose of such use;
5. the policies and practices of the agency regarding storage, retrievability, access controls, retention, and disposal of the records;
6. the title and business address of the agency official who is responsible for the system of records;
7. the agency procedures whereby a person can learn if the system contains a record pertaining to him;
8. the agency procedures whereby a person can find out how to gain access to any record pertaining to him contained in the system, and how he can contest its content;
9. the categories of sources or records in the system.

Federal agencies will usually send a copy of its annual notice upon request. A simple request should be addressed to the head of the agency.

Both the general and specific exemptions authorize agencies to exempt appropriate records from the provisions of items 7, 8, and 9. However, there is no exemption from the requirements of the first six items.[12] Thus, even the CIA, and all other agencies that maintain general- or specific-exemption records must provide public notice of the existence and general nature and structure of all record systems.

Does the Privacy Act limit the sources from which the government can collect information?

Yes, the Privacy Act requires that agencies collect information about a person from the person himself, as much as possible.[13] This section applies when the information affects an individual's rights, benefits, and privileges under federal programs.

This section is intended to limit the collection of information from third parties, not only because that information is less reliable, but also because the very process of interviewing neighbors, acquaintances, and employers is damaging to the individual. As described in the legislative history of the Privacy Act, this provision

> supports the principle that an individual should to the greatest extent possible be in control of information about him which is given to the government. This may not be practical in all cases for financial or logistical reasons or because of other statutory requirements. However, it is a principle designed to insure fairness in information collection which should be instituted wherever possible.[14]

General- and specific-exemption records may be excluded from this provision.

The act also requires that the agency inform each person whom it asks for information of (a) the authority for the collection of the information, (b) the principal purposes for which the information is intended to be used; (c) the "routine uses" of the information; and (d) the effects on the individual, if any, of not providing information.[15] Only general-exemption records may be excluded from this requirement; all agencies maintaining specific-exemption records must comply with this provision.

Are there any restrictions on the kinds of information that may be maintained in government files?

Yes. The Privacy Act has a number of requirements governing the maintenance of information about individuals.

First, it requires that agencies maintain only information that is relevant and necessary to accomplish a purpose required by statute or Executive Order.[16] This requirement is designed to insure that a federal agency weighs strongly the rights of personal privacy against its authority and need to gather personal information. Before an information-gathering program may be implemented, the agency must make a determination that its action is authorized and warranted to carry out a statutory [or Executive Order] obligation.[17]

Information is "necessary" for an agency purpose when "the needs of the agency and goals of the program cannot reasonably be met through alternative means."[18] Both general- and specific-exemption records can be excluded from this requirement.

In addition, the Privacy Act requires that an agency maintain all records that are used in making any determination about any person with such accuracy, relevance, timeliness, and completeness as is reasonably necessary to assure fairness to the person.[19] This provision, along with the limitation of records to relevant and necessary information, constitute the basic protections against misleading and prejudicial records that should not be maintained because they are either incorrect, irrelevant, outdated, or not thorough enough to be clear. Neither the Privacy Act nor the legislative history afford much insight into the interpretations of the standards of accuracy, relevance, timeliness, or completeness, and there has not yet been any significant judicial interpretation of this language. Moreover, the Privacy Act does not impose an absolute requirement that every bit of information be accurate, relevant, timely, and complete. Rather, the statute merely requires such adherence to those standards as will assure fairness to the individual.

Only general-exemption records can avoid the requirements of this provision; all specific-exemption records must fulfill the requirements.

The Privacy Act allows a person to seek amendment or correction of information which does not satisfy Privacy Act standards. In addition, a person may insert in the record a statement of disagreement which reflects the individual's objections. These procedures are discussed in the next chapter.

Can the government maintain records about an individual's lawful exercise of rights of speech and association?

No. The Privacy Act provides that an agency cannot maintain any record describing how anyone exercises rights guaranteed by the First Amendment.[20] However, such files can be maintained if (1) authorized by statute, (2) authorized by the individual or (3) if pertinent to and within the scope of an authorized law-enforcement activity.

The First Amendment guarantees the rights of free speech, press, association, and religious freedom. The implementing guidelines of the Office of Management and Budget, which apply throughout the government, state that in "determining whether or not a particular activity constitutes the exercise of a right guaranteed by the First Amendment, agencies will apply the broadest reasonable interpretation." [21] Although this section does not absolutely prohibit maintaining First Amendment information, it is clearly intended to give narrow limits to the information the government may maintain about a person's political, social, and religious activities.

The legislative history shows that this provision "is aimed at protecting Americans in the enjoyment of their thoughts, habits, attitudes, and beliefs in matters having nothing to do with the requirements of their dealings with an agency seeking information." [22] In addition, such information can be collected for law-enforcement purposes if it is pertinent to and within the scope of authorized law-enforcement activity. These limitations seem to prohibit the maintenance of information which was collected illegally.

The Privacy Act requires that *all* agencies abide by this prohibition against maintaining information on the exercise of First Amendment rights. There are no exemptions.

Does the Privacy Act govern the dissemination of information?

Yes. The Privacy Act contains detailed provisions limiting the conditions under which information about an individual may be disclosed or disseminated.

First, before disseminating any record about an individual to anyone other than a federal agency, the agency maintaining the record must make reasonable efforts to assure that such records are accurate, complete, timely, and relevant.[23] (This provision does not apply to releases made pursuant to the Freedom of Information Act.) This requirement is applicable to all agencies without exception.

Second, an agency may not disclose personally identifiable records "to any person, agency, or to another agency" except if the person who is the subject of the records requests the disclosure, or if that person consents in writing to the disclosure.[24] However, the general rule is substantially diluted by the provision that even without a request or consent, the record can be disclosed if it satisfies at least one of eleven specific authorizations for disclosure: [25]

1. To employees of that agency "who have a need for the record in the performance of their duties."
2. Pursuant to the Freedom of Information Act.
3. To the Bureau of the Census.
4. To a recipient who assures the agency that the information is to be used solely for statistical research and the information will not be personally identifiable.
5. To the National Archives
6. To any other government agency (including state and local governments) for civil or criminal law-enforcement activity, but only if the head of the agency specifically requests the information, identifying the purposes for which that information is sought.
7. In emergencies affecting the health or safety of the individual.
8. To either House of Congress.
9. To the Comptroller General in connection with the operations of the General Accounting Office.
10. Pursuant to court order.
11. For a "routine use."

The last is the broadest exception to the limitations on disclosure. The Privacy Act defines "routine use" as a "use of such record for a purpose which is compatible with the purpose for which it was collected." [26]

The routine-use provision was devised by Congress to avoid the need to specify each proper use of a record. "Routine use" is a flexible concept which requires only that the use be compatible, but not identical, with the use for which the record was collected.[27] Moreover, "routine" does not mean only the common uses but may include infrequent uses that are nonetheless compatible. Each agency is required to publish in the *Federal Register* a notice identifying each system of records including, among other things, each routine use of the records contained in the system, the categories of users, and the purpose of each such use.[28] In practical effect, an agency can make a use routine by saying so and then publishing that use in the *Federal Register*. Agencies may not exempt either general- or specific-exemption records from the disclosure provisions of the Privacy Act.

If a record is made available to another person or agency under legal compulsion, the agency must make reasonable effort to serve notice on the subject of the record when the process becomes a matter of public record.[29] Only general-exemption records may be excluded from this requirement.

Can a person find out if personal information has been disseminated outside the agency?

Yes.

The act requires each agency to keep an accurate accounting of (1) the date, nature, and purpose of each disclosure of a record to any person or to another agency, and (2) the name and address of the person or agency to whom the disclosure is made.[30] After the disclosure has been made, the accounting must be maintained for either five years or the life of the record, whichever is longer. Except for disclosures made to a law enforcement agency, the accounting of disclosures must be made available to the individual. Only general-exemption records may be excluded from the accounting provisions of the Privacy Act.

The accounting provisions serve three important functions: (1) they provide the record subject with a listing of the disclosures, and consequently some insight into the uses of the records; (2) they enable the agency to circulate corrections of those records to the users; and (3) they permit monitoring of agency procedures and compliance with the Privacy Act.[31]

Although the accounting provision is significant in

theory, it has not been effectively implemented by the agencies, probably because it is "widely regarded as the statute's single most burdensome provision" and has "little interest on the part of the general public." [32]

Since the accounting provision did not exist before the Privacy Act went into effect in September 1975, it is unlikely that an agency will have a record of disclosures made before then.

Does the Privacy Act provide any remedies for an agency's violation of the information-practices provisions?

Yes. An individual may bring a lawsuit challenging an agency's violation of Privacy Act information-practices provisions if the individual has suffered an adverse effect as a result of that violation. In addition to that general provision, the Privacy Act specifically authorizes a lawsuit when an agency makes an adverse determination about an individual based on a record which is inaccurate, irrelevant, untimely, or incomplete.[33]

In such lawsuits, the agency may be required to apply the information practices of the Privacy Act properly. For example, a suit may be brought to require an agency to remove inaccurate, irrelevant, untimely, or incomplete information, or information describing the exercise of a person's First Amendment rights.

Besides seeking the government's compliance with the information-practices provisions, the Privacy Act authorizes money damages in certain cases. In any suit brought against the government for violation of the information-practices provisions, if the court determines that the agency acted in a manner that was "intentional or willful," the United States shall be liable to the individual for (1) actual damages sustained by the individual as a result of the refusal or failure to comply with the Privacy Act (at least $1000) and (2) legal costs.[34]

A lawsuit may be brought in a U.S. District Court—either where the individual lives or has a principal place of business, where the agency keeps its records, or in the District of Columbia.[35] The action must be brought within two years of when the cause arises. If an agency materially or willfully misrepresents any information that is required to be disclosed to an individual, the action may be brought within two years after the individual's discovery of that misrepresentation.[36]

Finally, the Privacy Act specifically provides that an action may *not* be brought for any injury sustained as a result of a disclosure before its effective date, September 1975.[37]

NOTES

1. Fourth Annual Report of the President: Federal Personal Data Systems Subject to the Privacy Act of 1974, Calendar Year 1978, at page 7.
2. HALPERIN, THE LAWLESS STATE: THE CRIMES OF THE U.S. INTELLIGENCE AGENCIES (Penguin, 1976).
3. 5 U.S.C. §552a.
4. 5 U.S.C. §552a(a)(1) and (m).
5. 5 U.S.C. §552a(a)(3), (4), and (5).
6. Whalen v. Roe, 429 U.S. 435 (1976).
7. 5 U.S.C. §552a(j).
8. H.R. REP. NO. 1416, PRIVACY ACT 1974, 93rd Cong., 2d Sess. 19 (1974).
9. 5 U.S.C. §552a(k).
10. H.R. REP. *supra* note 8, at 20.
11. 5 U.S.C. §552a(e)(4).
12. 5 U.S.C. §552a(j) and (k).
13. 5 U.S.C. §552a(e)(2).
14. *Analysis of House and Senate Compromise Amendments to the Federal Privacy Act,* 120 CONG. REC. 40,405 (Dec. 17, 1974).
15. 5 U.S.C. §552a(e)(3). "Routine use" is described below in text accompanying footnote 25.
16. 5 U.S.C. §552a(e)(1).
17. S. REP. NO. 1183, PROTECTING INDIVIDUAL PRIVACY IN FEDERAL GATHERING, USE AND DISCLOSURE OF INFORMATION, 93rd Cong., 2d Sess. 45 (1974).
18. *Id.* at 46.
19. 5 U.S.C. §552a(e)(5).
20. 5 U.S.C. §552a(e)(7).
21. Office of Management and Budget, *Privacy Act Guidelines* §(e)(7), 40 Fed. Reg. 28,949, at 28,965 (1975).
22. S. REP., *supra* note 17, at 56.
23. 5 U.S.C. §552a(e)(6).
24. 5 U.S.C. §552a(b).
25. 5 U.S.C. §552a(b)(1)–(11).
26. 5 U.S.C. §552a(a)(7).

27. Office of Management and Budget, *Privacy Act Guidelines, supra* note 21, §(a)(7) at 28,953.
28. 5 U.S.C. §552a(e)(4)(D).
29. 5 U.S.C. §552a(e)(8).
30. 5 U.S.C. §552a(c).
31. Privacy Protection Study Commission, Personal Privacy in an Information Society 525 (July 1977).
32. *Id.*
33. 5 U.S.C. §§552a(g)(1)(C) and (D).
34. 5 U.S.C. §552a(g)(4).
35. 5 U.S.C. §552a(g)(5).
36. *Id.*
37. *Id.*

XIII

Electronic Surveillance

Can the government engage in electronic surveillance?

Yes, if it is done in accordance with the limitations of the Fourth Amendment to the Constitution and the requirements of federal statutory law.

The Fourth Amendment proclaims the "right of the people to be secure in their persons, houses, papers, and effects" and prohibits any government agency or official [1] from engaging in "unreasonable searches and seizures." It also provides that a court shall issue a "warrant" to search or seize only if the government shows "probable cause" and particularly describes "the place to be searched and the persons or things to be seized."

It is now well established that electronic surveillance is a search. It is, therefore, subject to the provisions of the Fourth Amendment—which means that, in most instances, a government wiretap is legal only if it is authorized by a warrant issued by a court. [2]

The federal government can obtain a warrant to engage in electronic surveillance only by satisfying the conditions and procedures prescribed by Title III of the Omnibus Crime Control and Safe Streets Act of 1968 (called Title III for brevity). [3] Although the Constitution restricts only government conduct, Title III governs electronic surveillance by private individuals or organizations as well.

What is meant by "electronic surveillance"?

"Electronic surveillance" means wiretapping or bugging. Those words are clear enough for most purposes, and will generally be used here. For the purposes of federal law, however, those words are not precise enough, so Title III refers to, and controls, the "interception of wire or oral communications."

A *wire communication* is a communication made partly

or completely through wire cable or other similar connections.[4] In addition, for the purposes of Title III, the communications facilities must be operated by a "common carrier"—that is, an enterprise in the business of interstate or foreign communication by wire or radio.[5] Thus, for example, a wire communication would include communication by any regular cable telephone connection, or any regular telephone communication with a mobile radiotelephone (because it is, in part, through a wire facility). Similarly, communications between two mobile radiotelephones through the facilities of a common carrier are covered. However, communications that do not use the wire facilities of a common carrier—such as direct contact between two walkie-talkies or an intercom connection in an office—are not wire communications; but they are covered under Title III as oral communications.

An *oral communication* is one made by a person apparently expecting that it is not subject to interception.[6] In this, it differs from a wire communication, which does not require any showing of an expectation of privacy. It is assumed that any wire communication—such as a telephone call—is made with an expectation of privacy.

Under the definition of oral communication, two elements must be present to show it should be covered by that statute. First, the speaker must exhibit an expectation of privacy. The Senate Report accompanying Title III says that the "person's expectation that his communication is or is not subject to 'interception' . . . is thus to be gathered and evaluated from and in terms of all the facts and circumstances."[7] It is likely, for example, that a person talking loudly in a public area will be held not to have shown the requisite interest in privacy; on the other hand, taking precautions to talk quietly behind closed doors to a restricted audience may be sufficient. Between these two extremes are an infinite number of variations, each of which must be analyzed in the light of all the circumstances. Second, the speaker's expectation of privacy must be justified. This overlaps with the first criterion and involves an examination of all the surrounding circumstances such as where, how, when, and to whom the communication was made.

Title III prohibits the interception of any wire or oral communication except in accordance with the specific requirements of the statute. An "interception" is defined to mean any overhearing of any wire or oral communication through the use of any "electronic, mechanical, or other device."[8] This includes *any* device which can intercept a wire or oral communication.[9] The statute excludes a hearing aid, any telephone or telegraph equipment furnished to and being used by a subscriber (such as an extension telephone), or any such equipment being used in the ordinary course of business by the telephone company or law-enforcement officer.

The legislative history of Title III emphasizes that Congress sought to protect the privacy of the *content* of communications and not the fact that a communication took place. Thus, Title III protects the content of the telephone conversation itself, but not telephone-company toll records, even though those records may disclose information about the conversation. Similarly, Title III does not prevent the tracing of phone calls without actually overhearing the conversation.[10] The Supreme Court has held that the use of a pen register, a device that detects the telephone number called but does not intrude in the actual communication, is not covered by Title III.[11]

Can any government official seek a warrant to intercept communications?

No. Title III directs that only the Attorney General, or a specially designated Assistant Attorney General, may authorize an application to a federal judge for a warrant for a wiretap to intercept communications.[12] The law "centralizes in a publicly responsible official subject to the political process the formulation of law enforcement policy on the use of electronic surveillance techniques." Congress intended to "avoid the possibility that divergent practices might develop" and, if "abuses occur, the lines of responsibility lead to an identifiable person."[13] The Supreme Court has held that the requirement of personal approval "was intended to play a central role in the statutory scheme" and that, therefore, a wiretap that was authorized by an executive assistant to the Attorney General was illegal.[14]

The statute also requires that the application be limited to proposed wiretaps by the Federal Bureau of Investigation or another federal agency responsible for investigating the offense for which the wiretap is sought.[15]

Title III also permits the "principal prosecuting attorney" of any state, or any political subdivision of a state, to apply to a state-court judge for an order authorizing a wiretap—but only if the prosecutor is specifically authorized to do so by state statute.[16]

Virtually every state has enacted its own law which prescribes procedures for obtaining a wiretap warrant and the conditions under which it may be done. The state statutes are generally similar to, but do not necessarily mirror, the federal law. Throughout the discussion of the federal wiretap law, only general reference will be made to the various state laws. The reader interested in the details of state requirements and procedures must consult the law of the particular state.

It will usually not be difficult to locate the applicable state law in the compilation of state statutes found in any law library. In the federal statutes, the law is indexed under the headings "communications," "interception" and "wiretapping." Similar index references will probably be found in the state statutes. In addition, a lawyer or law librarian may be able to provide a specific citation for the statute. If all else fails, the office of the state Attorney General may provide the relevant citations.

Can the government intercept communications for any reason?

No. The wiretap must be intended only for obtaining evidence of *designated offenses*—certain federal crimes enumerated by Congress. The designated offenses fall into three somewhat overlapping categories:

1. *National security offenses:* crimes relating to nuclear secrets punishable by imprisonment for more than one years; espionage, sabotage; treason.
2. *Intrinsically serious offenses:* murder; kidnapping; robbery; riots; assassination and assault on the President or members of Congress; and drug-related offenses.
3. *Offenses characteristic of organized crime:* improper payments and loans to labor organizations; extortion; bribery or improper influence of public officials and witnesses; bribery in sporting contests; unlawful use

of explosives; obstruction of criminal investigations; obstruction of state or local law enforcement; interference with commerce by threats or violence; interstate and foreign travel or transportation in aid of racketeering enterprises; offer, acceptance, or solicitation to influence operations of employee-benefit plan; gambling enterprises; theft from interstate shipment; embezzlement from pension and welfare funds; interstate transportation of stolen property; violations with respect to racketeer-influenced and corrupt organizations: counterfeiting; bankruptcy fraud; extortionate credit transactions.[17]

In addition, a warrant to intercept communications may be sought for *conspiracy* to commit any of the designated offenses.

If authorized by state statute, the appropriate prosecuting attorneys in the state may seek a warrant to obtain evidence of the several state offenses—murder, kidnapping, gambling, robbery, bribery, extortion, dealing in narcotic drugs, marijuana or other dangerous drugs, or other crimes dangerous to life, limb, or property, and punishable by imprisonment for more than one year—if these crimes are designated in a state statute authorizing such interception. A warrant can also be sought for conspiracy to commit any of the designated state offenses.

What information must be included in an application for a wiretap warrant?

A. Each application must be made in writing and upon oath to the court, and it must contain certain information detailing the facts of the case and the need to intercept communications.

The Fourth Amendment authorizes a warrant to be issued only upon a showing of *probable cause*. A number of Supreme Court cases have established the minimum requirements for such a showing of probable cause in cases involving wiretaps. For example, in *Berger* v. *New York*[18] the court reversed a state bribery conviction because the government had placed a recording device in the defendants office pursuant to a state law which did not provide adequate judicial supervision, or protective procedures. And in *Katz* v. *United States*[19] the Supreme

Court held that an electronic bug attached to the outside of a telephone booth, without court approval violated the defendant's Fourth Amendment rights.

In order to permit the court to determine if the government has sufficient justification, under the Fourth Amendment, to intercept a communication, Title III requires [20] that each application contain:

1. *The identities of the law-enforcement officers making and authorizing the application.* The purpose of this provision is simply to fix responsibility.

2. *A complete statement of the facts justifying the application, including (a) details as to the particular offense under investigation, (b) a particular description of the nature and location of the facilities or place where the communication is to be intercepted, (c) a description of the type of communications to be intercepted, and (d) the identity of the person, if known, committing the offense and whose communications are to be intercepted.* This provision is designed to satisfy the constitutional requirement that the government detail the facts supporting its application for a warrant. Indeed the Fourth Amendment itself requires that a warrant shall not issue unless "particularly describing the place to be searched. . . ." The Supreme Court has specifically applied this constitutional command to governmental eavesdropping.[21] With respect to the requirement that the application include the "identity of the person, if known" the Supreme Court has held in *United States* v. *Donovan* that the government cannot list only its principal targets. The application must identify every individual, whether or not a principal target, if (a) the government has probable cause to believe that person is engaged in the criminal conduct under investigation and (b) the government expects to intercept that person's communication over the target telephone, whether or not the individual is the owner of the target telephone and whether or not the government expects the individual to use the target telephone for incoming or outgoing communications.[22]

3. *A complete statement as to whether or not other investigative procedures have been tried and have failed or why they reasonably appear to be unlikely to succeed if tried or to be too dangerous.* The Supreme Court has recognized that "[f]ew threats to liberty exist which are greater than that posed by the use of eavesdropping devices." [23] Congress intended that it not be lightly employed. Other investigative procedures include visual surveillance, questioning or interrogation of suspects under grant of immunity, and the use of regular search warrants. In its standards for deciding whether the government has made the proper showing of need, Congress recognized that the "judgment would involve consideration of all the facts and circumstances." [24]

4. *A statement of the period of time for which the interception must be maintained, including, if the interception is not to end automatically when the described communication is obtained, a statement of facts establishing probable cause to believe that additional communications of the same type will occur thereafter.* Coupled with other provisions of Title III, this provision is meant to insure that an interception is not conducted for any longer than is necessary. In *Berger*, the Supreme Court compared an unnecessarily lengthy governmental eavesdropping to a general search warrant, which is constitutionally prohibited.[25]

5. *A complete statement of the facts concerning all previous applications for authorization to intercept the communications of the same person or at the same facilities.* This provision requires the judge to be informed of previous wiretap applications in order to avoid abuses that might result if the government tried to "shop around" for a judge willing to grant its application.

The court may also require the government to furnish additional testimony or evidence in support of its application.[26]

The information required in a federal application for a warrant to intercept communications must also be included in an application made by a state official under state law. However, state law may have stricter requirements than federal law.

Is a court required to issue a warrant to intercept communications that has been applied for by the government?
No. The court is not permitted to issue a warrant unless it determines that the application satisfies all of the constitutional and statutory prerequisites. Even then, the law does not require the judge to authorize the interception. He may independently judge whether the proposed wiretap is proper and suitable in the circumstances of the particular case.[27]

To grant an application, the court *must* decide that:

1. there is probable cause to believe that an individual will imminently be engaged in a designated offense— that is, an offense for which eavesdropping is authorized;
2. there is probable cause to believe that communications about that offense will be obtained through the interception;
3. normal investigative techniques have been tried and have failed or are unlikely to succeed, or are too dangerous;
4. there is probable cause to believe that the facilities to be intercepted are leased to, listed in the name of, or commonly used by the subject of the wiretap.

This provision of Title III is meant to implement the Fourth Amendment command that a warrant shall be issued only upon a showing of "probable cause." The Supreme Court has concluded in a case dealing with governmental eavesdropping that probable cause under the Fourth Amendment exists when the known facts and circumstances are based on reasonably trustworthy information and are sufficient to warrant a man of reasonable caution to believe the fact in question.[28] As a result of the Title III requirement that the court make specific findings of probable cause, "the order will link a specific person, specific offense, and specific place. Together they are intended to meet the test of the Constitution that electronic surveillance techniques be used only under the most precise and discriminate circumstances which fully comply with the requirement of particularity." [29]

To satisfy the Constitution, an order authorizing the wiretap must specify:

1. the identity of the person, if known, whose communications are to be intercepted;
2. the nature and location of the communications facilities for which, or the place where, authority to intercept is granted;
3. a particular description of the type of communication sought to be intercepted, and a statement of the particular offense to which it relates;
4. the identity of the agency authorized to intercept the communications, and of the person authorizing the application;
5. the period of time during which such interception is authorized, including a statement as to whether or not the interception shall automatically terminate when the described communication has been first obtained.[30]

Applicable state statutes are not permitted to authorize a wiretap on any lesser standards than required by the federal law, but if the state law is stricter, state officials are bound by those standards.

For how long may a court authorize a wiretap?

The initial period may not exceed thirty days or the period necessary to achieve the objective of the wiretap, whichever is shorter.[31]

The court is authorized to order successive thirty-day extensions of the original order, but only upon the filing of a new application (which must satisfy all the statutory requirements for original applications) and only if the court makes new findings (according to the same provisions required for original determinations) for each thirty-day extension.

Every original order and extension must provide that the interception shall take place as soon as practicable and that it must immediately terminate after its objective is achieved.

Does the government have to notify a person whose communications were intercepted pursuant to a court order?

Yes. However, the notification procedures are not very strict and may be avoided in certain cases.

Title III provides that interception applications and court orders are to be "sealed" by the court, which means that the papers are not part of the public record and are not available for examination.[32] Therefore, a person who suspects that communications are being intercepted is not able to go to the court and check the records.

The statute does require that the persons named in the interception application or order must receive an "inventory" within a reasonable time, but not exceeding ninety days after the termination of the interception (or denial of an application to intercept communications).[33] They must be given notice of

1. the fact of the entry of the order or the application;
2. the date of the entry of the order; and, if interception was authorized, the period of time allowed;
3. the fact that during the period communications were or were not intercepted.

Furthermore, the statute provides that the court, at its discretion, may direct that similar notice be provided to any other parties to intercepted communications "in the interest of justice." The Supreme Court has held that the government has a duty to provide the judge with relevant information about the other parties whose communications were intercepted so that the judge can decide if additional notice should be given.[34]

If the government has "good cause," the statute permits it to make a motion, without notifying the subjects, to postpone sending these notices.

Are these notification procedures adequate?

The Title III notification procedures are inadequate and cannot be relied on to provide meaningful notice and information to everyone whose communications were intercepted. First, although the notice is called an "inventory," it need include nothing more than the fact that a wiretap order was entered, the period of the wiretap, and whether communications were overheard. This should be compared to the "inventory" provided in a conventional search, which informs the subject what was taken.[35]

Second, the statute does not require notice to *all* people whose communications were intercepted. Only the individuals named in the application or order must receive notice; other people who may have been overheard, even if they are identifiable, may receive notice only at the court's discretion.

Third, the statute requires service of the notice "within a reasonable time but not later than ninety days" after the termination of the interception. Although the ninety-day period was clearly intended to establish the maximum limits of the reasonable period for notice, as a practical matter ninety days has become the minimum notice period, because courts have freely authorized the postponement of notice upon request by the government.

Are there emergency situations in which the government may intercept communications without a court order?

Yes. In certain very limited situations the government may execute an emergency interception of communications without a court order.[36] It may be executed by any investigative or law-enforcement official specially designated by the Attorney General. The official must reasonably determine that there are grounds for an order to authorize such interception. That is to say, the official must conclude that, if this were not an emergency and the full procedures of Title III had to be employed, there would be grounds for the court to grant the application to intercept communications. He must also reasonably determine that the interception will take place before it would be possible, "with due diligence," to obtain an order authorizing it.

Such emergency interceptions cannot be undertaken for all designated offenses.[37] They are limited to two categories: conspiratorial activities (1) threatening the national security or (2) characteristic of organized crime. Congress was concerned that meetings of conspirators are often "set up and the place finally chosen almost simultaneously" and that "requiring a court order in these situations would be tantamount to failing to authorize the surveillance." [38]

An emergency interception must be followed within forty-eight hours by an application for court approval. In the absence of an order, it must immediately terminate when the communication sought has been obtained or when the application for approval is denied, whichever is earlier.

If the application for court approval is denied, or if the interception is terminated without the government ever getting a court order, the contents must be treated as having been obtained in violation of Title III.[39]

How does the government obtain access to the facilities to be intercepted?

Title III permits a court to order any person to cooperate with the installation of interception equipment. In addition, government officials may enter private premises in order to place, service, or remove equipment.

If the government obtains approval to intercept communications, it may also seek a court order requiring others to provide any necessary assistance. A court may order a communication company, landlord, custodian, or other person to furnish the government with information, facilities, and technical assistance so that the interception may be accomplished unobtrusively and without alerting the subject.[40] Even without a court order, it is not unlawful for a communication company to provide information, facilities, or technical assistance to any law-enforcement officer authorized to intercept communications.[41] Any person furnishing facilities or assistance shall be compensated at "prevailing rates." [42]

The Supreme Court has concluded that an order authorizing the interception of communications implicitly includes the power to break into the subject's premises in order to install, service, or remove the interception device.[43] The government does *not* have to obtain separate approval from the judge for the break-in. Of course, many interceptions, especially telephone wiretaps, can be made through central facilities without a break-in at all.

Can the government record intercepted communications?

Yes. In fact, Title III requires recording if possible.[44] The recording must be made in such a way as to protect it from editing or obliteration. The tapes must be maintained for at least ten years. The apparent purpose of this provision is to protect both the government and the individual by insuring that the record of an intercepted communications is accurate, that the recording is not tampered with and that the recording is available for admission as evidence in court proceedings.[45]

May the government disclose the intercepted communications?

Yes, but only if expressly authorized by Title III.

Title III allows a law-enforcement officer who has obtained information by means of an authorized interception to disclose that information to another law-enforcement officer, but only to the extent that the disclosure is appropriate to the performance of the official duties of either officer.[46] This provision is meant to encourage "close Federal, State and local cooperation in the administration of justice." [47]

The statute also authorizes the disclosure of intercepted communications "to the extent such use is appropriate to the proper performance" of the duties of the law-enforcement officer who has obtained the information.[48] This provision is meant to allow disclosure to establish probable cause for arrest, to establish probable cause to search, or to develop witnesses.

The statute also authorizes disclosure by a law-enforcement officer "while giving testimony under oath . . . in any proceeding held under the authority of the United States or of any State or political subdivision thereof." [49] This provision is intended to permit disclosure at a trial to establish guilt directly, to corroborate or impeach a witness, or to refresh the recollection of a witness.

Can the government use information about crimes which were not identified in the order authorizing the interception of communications?

Yes. Title III provides that when a law-enforcement officer intercepts communications about an offense other than those specified in the order (even if that other offense is not a "designated offense" and therefore could not, itself, be used as a basis for the interception) that evidence can be disclosed in the exercise of official duties and to other law-enforcement officers having an official need to know.[50]

The evidence may be disclosed by the law-enforcement

officer while giving testimony, but only if the court rules, upon motion by the government, that the communication was otherwise properly intercepted in accordance with the provisions of Title III. The government must show that the original order was lawfully obtained, that it was sought in good faith and not as a subterfuge search, and that the communication was incidentally intercepted during the course of a lawfully executed order.[51]

In addition, information obtained from an interception about a person not previously known as a target of the wiretap may be used against that person even though not named in the application and order. Title III requires the interception application and court order to identify the person whose communications are to be intercepted only if the identity is known.[52] However, if the authorities did not have probable cause to believe the individual was engaged in the criminal activities being investigated or they did not expect the individual to be using the targeted facilities, the application and order need not name that person.

Can the government intercept "privileged communications," such as those between attorney and client or husband and wife?

Yes. Title III does not prohibit the interception of privileged communications.

However, Title III provides that a privileged communication that is intercepted "shall not lose its privileged character."[53] Therefore, although the law does not prohibit the interception of the privileged communications, it allows an individual the right to object to the disclosure or use of the information intercepted.

Title III does not create any privileges. Congress recognized that the "existence and scope of the four generally recognized privileges (attorney-client, physician-patient, clergyman-confidant and husband-wife) varies from jurisdiction to jurisdiction."[54] Therefore, the determination of what constitutes a privileged communication, and whether the intercepted communication satisfies the prerequisites for a privilege, must be separately determined in each jurisdiction.

Some state statutes preclude the interception of privileged communications by prohibiting the government from interfering with facilities likely to be used for privileged communication, or by requiring the interception to shut down during the privileged communication.

Can the government intercept communications that do not pertain to any criminal conduct?

Yes, but only if ancillary to an authorized interception focusing on criminal conduct—and even then the government must try to minimize the unrelated interceptions.

Title III requires that "the authorization to intercept . . . shall be conducted in such a way as to minimize the interception of communications not otherwise subject to interception. . . ." [55] The so-called "minimization requirement" derives from the Fourth Amendment prohibition against general searches—that is, searches which are merely fishing expeditions for incriminating evidence. In *Berger* v. *New York*,[56] the Supreme Court struck down a New York wiretapping statute which the Court disapprovingly described as allowing unlimited interception of all conversations covered by the wiretap "indiscriminately and without regard to their connection to the crime under investigation." The Supreme Court explained in *Berger* that the minimization requirement is designed "to prevent improper invasion of the right of privacy provided by the Fourth Amendment and to curtail the indiscriminate seizure of communications."

In *Scott* v. *United States* [57] the Supreme Court recently analyzed the Title III minimization requirement. In that case, the government agents admitted that they made no effort to minimize the interceptions, even though the court order required minimization, and 60 percent of the intercepted communications did not pertain to criminal conduct.

The Supreme Court ruled that the government's failure to minimize did not, in itself, make the interceptions unreasonable. The essential issue is whether the interception of the noncriminal communications was reasonable, entirely apart from whether the agents intended to minimize. That is to say, even if the agent intentionally violated the order by not minimizing the interceptions, the court will look to the interceptions themselves to see if they were proper.

The court identified a number of reasons why even an

agent intending to minimize the interceptions might intercept noncriminal communications. For example:

1. Nonpertinent calls may be short (e.g., calls to persons who couldn't come to the phone, wrong numbers) thus making it difficult for the agent to make the necessary judgments about relevance before the call was completed.
2. Nonpertinent calls may be one time only, which do not allow the agent to fit the conversation within a category of innocent communications which should not be intercepted.
3. Nonpertinent calls may involve guarded or coded language which is only later determined to be irrelevant.

It is also necessary, according to the Supreme Court to consider the circumstances of the wiretap:

4. An investigation of a widespread conspiracy may require more extensive surveillance in an attempt to determine the precise scope of the enterprise.
5. The type of use to which the telephone is usually put may influence minimization requirements (e.g., greater minimization may be required for interceptions at a public pay phone than a private business phone).
6. During early stages of the interception period greater latitude may be necessary than at later stages because of the need to determine which communications are nonpertinent.

All of the considerations that determine the reasonableness of an interception must be analyzed in terms of the particular facts of each case. There is no general formula that will decide every case.

Can a private individual (not associated with the government in any way) legally intercept communications?
No. With limited exceptions pertaining only to functions of the Federal Communications Commission (FCC) and the operation of telephone-company equipment, Title III prohibits private individuals or organizations from intercepting communications. Furthermore, Title III generally prohibits the manufacture and sale of interception devices

and authorizes the government to seize such devices if transported or used in interstate commerce.

Title III makes it a crime for anyone to intercept, attempt to intercept, or solicit anybody else to intercept wire communications, except in accordance with court-ordered wiretaps authorized by Title III. The crime is punishable by not more than a $10,000 fine and five years' imprisonment.[58]

It is also a crime, similarly punishable, to use any device or apparatus to intercept wire communications. In order to establish federal jurisdiction, the crime of using an interception device must also include the charge that (1) the device is affixed to a telephone connection, (2) the device transmits by radio, (3) the device is known to have been sent through the mail or transported in interstate commerce, (4) the device is used on the premises of, or for the purposes of obtaining information from, any business engaged in interstate commerce, or (5) the person using the device acts in the District of Columbia, Puerto Rico, or any other territory or possession.

It is a comparable crime to disclose or use the contents of communications which were known (or should have been known) to have been obtained by interceptions in violation of Title III.

The statute provides that it is *not* unlawful:

1. For a telephone-company employee to intercept, disclose, or use communications in the normal course of his employment while engaged in any activity which is necessary to the rendition of his service or the protection of the rights or property of the telephone company. (However, the telephone company may not utilize "service observing or random monitoring except for mechanical or service quality control checks.")

2. For the telephone company to provide information, facilities, or technical assistance to a law-enforcement officer who is authorized to engage in a wiretap pursuant to Title III.

3. For an employee of the FCC to intercept and disclose communications transmitted by radio if it is in the normal course of the employment and is undertaken as part of the FCC's monitoring duties.[59]

Finally, it is *not* unlawful for any person to intercept a communication where such person is a party to the communication or one of the parties has given prior consent to the interception. However, even such private interceptions are forbidden if done for the purpose of committing any illegal or other injurious act.[60]

In order to prevent the unlawful interception of communications, Title III makes it a crime to send through the mail or to transport in interstate commerce any device which is primarily useful for surreptitious interception of communications. The crime is punishable by not more than $10,000 fine and five years' imprisonment.[61] It is a similar crime (1) to manufacture, possess, or sell any such device if it is known, or it should have been known, that the device (or any component of the device) was sent through the mail or transported in interstate commerce, and (2) to place an advertisement for any such device in any publication which will be sent through the mails or transported in interstate commerce.

It is however, *not* lawful to send through the mail, transport in interstate commerce, manufacture, possess, or sell any such device *if* it is done by an employee of a communications company in the normal course of business or by an employee of any level of government in the normal course of that government's business.[62].

Any device which is used, sent, manufactured, possessed, sold, or advertised in violation of Title III may be seized and forfeited to the United States.[63] Of course, seizures and forfeitures must comply with the Fourth Amendment and applicable statutory law.

Can the government ever intercept communications without a court order?

Yes. Title III authorizes the government to intercept communications without a warrant in narrowly prescribed emergency situations.[64] Also, a government official may intercept a communication if he is a party to the communication, or where one of the parties has given prior consent.

In addition, the President may have some inherent power to intercept communications without a warrant in a limited category of "national security" cases. Although Title III expressly states that it does not apply to the exercise of presidential power, the Constitution itself limits the President. Title III states[65] that it does not limit the "constitutional power of the President" to "take such measures as he deems necessary" to:

1. protect the nation against actual or potential attack or other hostile acts of a foreign power;
2. obtain foreign-intelligence information deemed essential to the security of the United States;
3. protect national-security information against foreign intelligence activities;
4. protect the United States against the overthrow of the government by force or other unlawful means;
5. protect the United States against any other clear and present danger to the structure or existence of the government.

The Supreme Court has concluded that Title III does not confer any power on the President. The statute merely provides that it should not be interpreted to limit or disturb whatever power the President may have with respect to designated national security interests. "In short, Congress simply left presidential powers where it found them." [66]

Even though Title III does not apply to the exercise of presidential powers with respect to national-security and certain internal-security matters, the Supreme Court has recognized that the Fourth Amendment *does* limit those powers. In *United States* v. *United States District Court*,[67] the Supreme Court held that when acting to protect the nation's internal security, the government must obtain prior judicial approval for any interception of communications (or, in fact, any other search or seizure) of a United States citizen or domestic organization, not an agent of a foreign power. The Supreme Court explicitly declined to decide whether the President would also have to obtain a warrant in cases involving foreign powers or their agents.

In the espionage investigation of David Truong and Donald Humphrey,[68] the government intercepted communications without a warrant, relying on the President's inherent powers to protect the national security against threats from foreign governments or their agents or spies. At the trial, the district court approved the warrantless interception of communications in espionage cases. Other courts, including two courts of appeal, have sanctioned warrantless interception in national-security cases involving the agents of foreign powers.[69] However, in a case involving the interception of communications of a domestic organization but where the government asserted the presidential power to engage in foreign-intelligence-gathering for the protection of national security, the District of Columbia Court of Appeals required the government to obtain a warrant.[70] Thus far, the Supreme Court has refused to review any of the court-of-appeals decisions which deal with the President's power to authorize warrantless interceptions in national-security cases involving foreign nationals or agents, although the Court may decide to review the Truong-Humphrey conviction.

Title III also authorizes warrantless interceptions when a government official is party to the communication or where at least one of the parties to communication has given prior consent to the interception.[71] This provision of Title III reflects existing law as developed by the Supreme Court. For example, the Court has ruled that it is not a violation of the Fourth Amendment for government agents to intercept communications by monitoring a hidden transmitter concealed on an informant. The informant was a party to the conversation and thus since "the law gives no protection to the wrongdoer whose trusted accomplice is or becomes a police informer, neither should it protect him when that same agent has recorded or transmitted the conversations. . . ."[72] Similarly, the Court has held that it was not illegal for a police officer to listen in on an extension telephone to a conversation with the consent of one of the people in the conversation.[73]

Finally, the legislative history of Title III indicates that "consent," for the purposes of this provision, "may be express or implied. Surveillance devices in banks or apartment houses for institutional or personal protection would be impliedly consented to."[74]

Does a person have any remedies for the illegal interception of communications?

Yes. A person may bring a civil action against any person who intercepts communications in violation of Title III. If the government intercepts communications in violation of Title III, the evidence obtained may be suppressed—

that is, the government may not be able to use that information against the individual in a criminal proceeding.

Title III provides that any person whose communications are intercepted, disclosed, or used in violation of Title III shall be entitled to bring a civil action against the person who violated the statute.[75] If the plaintiff is able to demonstrate that the defendant intercepted, disclosed, or used the communication in violation of the statute, the plaintiff is entitled to recover the amount of actual damages suffered, but not less than $100 a day for each day of violation or $1,000, whichever is higher, and punitive damages. The plaintiff is also entitled to recover reasonable litigation costs and attorney's fees. Under the civil-damages provision of Title III the plaintiff may sue *any* person— even a government official—who engages in prohibited conduct. The plaintiff does not have to prove that the defendant acted with malice or in bad faith. However, the defendant's good-faith reliance on a court order or legislative authorization "shall constitute a complete defense to any civil or criminal action brought under this chapter or under any other law." [76]

In addition to civil remedies, a person whose communications have been illegally intercepted may be able to prevent the government from using the evidence it has obtained. Entirely apart from Title III, the federal courts have employed the so-called "exclusionary rule" to *suppress* illegally obtained evidence—that is, to prohibit the government from using illegally obtained evidence against a criminal defendant. The exclusionary rule has been the subject of extensive consideration by the courts, which have defined and refined its scope in the context of countless factual circumstances. A general discussion of the exclusionary rule is beyond the scope of this book; however, Title III contains both substantive and procedural provisions affecting the suppression of evidence obtained from the illegal interception of communications.

Title III provides that the contents of an intercepted communication, or evidence derived from such interception, may not be received in evidence at any trial or hearing if the disclosure would violate the statute.[77] As described earlier in this chapter, the disclosure of intercepted information in a trial or hearing is permitted only if the interception was made in accordance with the provisions of Title III.

Title III also details the procedures by which an individual may seek to suppress evidence obtained from an interception of communications. Any "aggrieved person" may make a suppression motion, but the motion must be made before the trial or hearing unless there was no opportunity to do so or the person was not aware of the grounds for the motion.[78] The statute defines an *aggrieved person* as a person who was a party to an intercepted communication or a person against whom the interception was directed.[79] Generally, this means that only a person whose communications were intercepted or whose telephone was tapped may move to suppress the evidence obtained.[80]

A person may make a motion to suppress evidence obtained from an intercepted communication on the following grounds:

1. That the communication was unlawfully intercepted.
2. That the court order authorizing the interception was insufficient on its face.
3. That the interception was not made in conformity with the court's authorization order.[81]

The Supreme Court has considered the interpretation of this provision on a number of occasions. In *United States* v. *Giordano*,[82] the government had intercepted communications based upon the approval of an Executive Assistant to the Attorney General, rather than by the Attorney General or a specially designated Assistant Attorney General, as required by Title III.[83] In holding that the evidence should be suppressed, the Court ruled that "Congress intended to require suppression, where there is a failure to satisfy any of those statutory requirements that *directly and substantially implement* the congressional intention to limit the use of intercept procedures to those situations clearly calling for the employment of this extraordinary investigative device." [84] Since the Court concluded that preapplication approval by officials at the highest level of government "was intended to play a central role in the statutory scheme, . . . suppression must follow when it is shown that this statutory requirement has been ignored." [85]

However, the Supreme Court very quickly made clear

that not every violation of the statute warranted suppression of the evidence. In *United States* v. *Chavez*,[86] the interception application was, in fact, authorized by the Attorney General. However the application erroneously identified an Assistant Attorney General as the authorizing official. The court ruled that the "misidentification of the officer authorizing the wiretap application did not affect the fulfillment of any of the reviewing or approval functions required by Congress. . . ." [87] Therefore, the interception was not "unlawful" within the meaning of the suppression provision of Title III. In a later case,[88] the Supreme Court held that the government's failure to identify all subjects of the interception properly [89] and its failure to comply with the discretionary inventory requirements [90] were both violations of the statute but not sufficiently central in the statutory scheme to warrant suppression.

In summary, the Supreme Court has directed courts to examine a variety of factors to determine whether a violation of Title III should result in the suppression of interception evidence: (1) whether the provision plays a central role in any aspect of the procedural scheme of Title III; (2) whether the violation actually affected the functioning of the officials required to execute the provisions of Title III; (3) whether the violation resulted in an interception which would not otherwise occur if the government had strictly complied with the provisions of Title III; and (4) whether the individual who was affected by the violation suffered any actual harm.

The suppression of evidence involves complex and still developing principles of law. Any person who finds himself in a proceeding involving the use of intercepted communications should be assisted by counsel.

NOTES

1. The Fourth Amendment specifically applies to the federal government. The Fourteenth Amendment makes the Fourth Amendment applicable to state and local governments as well.
2. At present, only the so-called "national security" electronic surveillance may not be subject to the warrant requirement. See discussion in text accompanying footnote.

3. 18 U.S.C. §§2510–2520.
4. 18 U.S.C. §2510(1).
5. 18 U.S.C. §2510(10); 47 U.S.C. §153(h).
6. 18 U.S.C. §2510(2).
7. S. REP. No. 1097, 90th Cong., 2d Sess., cited in 1968 U.S. CODE, CONG. AND ADMIN. NEWS 2177 *et seq.*, 2178 (hereinafter "S. REP.," with page number reference to the U.S. CODE CONG. AND ADMIN. NEWS).
8. 18 U.S.C. §2510(4).
9. 18 U.S.C. §2510(5).
10. S. REP. at 2178.
11. United States v. New York Telephone Co., 434 U.S. 159 (1977).
12. 18 U.S.C. §2516(1).
13. S. REP. at 2185.
14. United States v. Giordano, 416 U.S. 505, 528 (1974).
15. 18 U.S.C. §2516(1).
16. 18 U.S.C. §2516(2).
17. 18 U.S.C. §2516(1).
18. 388 U.S. 41 (1967).
19. 389 U.S. 347 (1967).
20. 18 U.S.C. §2518(1).
21. Berger v. New York, 388 U.S. 41, 58–60 (1967); Katz v. United States, 389 U.S. 345, 354–56 (1967).
22. 429 U.S. 413 (1977).
23. Berger v. New York, 388 U.S. 63 (1967).
24. S. REP. at 2190.
25. 388 U.S. at 59.
26. 18 U.S.C. §2518(2).
27. 18 U.S.C. §2518(3).
28. Berger v. New York, 388 U.S. 55 (1967).
29. S. REP. at 2191.
30. 18 U.S.C. §2518(4).
31. 18 U.S.C. 2518(5).
32. 18 U.S.C. §2518(8)(b).
33. 18 U.S.C. §2518(8)(d).
34. United States v. Donovan, 429 U.S. 413 (1977).
35. FED. R. CRIM. P. 41(d).
36. 18 U.S.C. §2518(7).
37. The designated offenses are described in the text accompanying footnote 17.
38. S. REP. at 2193.
39. 18 U.S.C. §2518(7). The effect of interceptions that are obtained in violation of Title III is discussed in the text accompanying footnote 74.
40. 18 U.S.C. §2518(4); United States v. New York Telephone Co., 434 U.S. 159 (1977).
41. 18 U.S.C. §2511(2)(a)(ii).

42. 18 U.S.C. §2518(4).
43. Dalia v. United States, 60 L.Ed.2d 177 (1979).
44. 18 U.S.C. §2518(8)(a).
45. S. REP. at 2193.
46. 18 U.S.C. §2517(1).
47. S. REP. at 2188.
48. 18 U.S.C. §2517(2).
49. 18 U.S.C. §2517(3).
50. 18 U.S.C. §2517(5).
51. S. REP. at 2185.
52. See discussion in text accompanying footnote 22.
53. 18 U.S.C. §2517(4).
54. S. REP. at 2189.
55. 18 U.S.C. §2518(5).
56. 388 U.S. 41 (1967).
57. 436 U.S. 128 (1978).
58. 18 U.S.C. §2511.
59. 18 U.S.C. §2511(2).
60. 18 U.S.C. §2511(3).
61. 18 U.S.C. §2512.
62. 18 U.S.C. §2512(2).
63. 18 U.S.C. §2513.
64. Emergency interceptions are discussed in text accompany-
    ing footnote 36.
65. 18 U.S.C. §2511(3).
66. United States v. United States District Court, 407 U.S.
    297, 303 (1972).
67. Id.
68. United States v. Humphrey, 456 F.Supp. 51 (E.D.Va.
    1978).
69. United States v. Butenko, 494 F.2d 593 (3rd Cir.) (en
    banc), cert. denied 419 U.S. 881 (1974); United States v.
    Brown, 484 F.2d 418 (6th Cir. 1973).
70. Zweibon v. Mitchell, 516 F.2d 594 (D.C. Cir. 1975).
71. 18 U.S.C. §2511(2)(c).
72. United States v. White, 401 U.S. 745 (1971).
73. Rathburn v. United States, 355 U.S. 107 (1957).
74. S. REP. at 2182.
75. 18 U.S.C. §2520.
76. Id.
77. 18 U.S.C. §2515.
78. 18 U.S.C. §2518(10).
79. 18 U.S.C. §2510(11).
80. Alderman v. United States, 394 U.S. 165 (1969).
81. 18 U.S.C. §2518(10).
82. 416 U.S. 505 (1974).
83. 18 U.S.C. §2516.

84. United States v. Giordano, 416 U.S. at 527 (emphasis added).
85. *Id.* at 528.
86. 416 U.S. 562 (1974).
87. *Id.* at 575.
88. United States v. Donovan, 429 U.S. 413 (1977).
89. The identification requirement is contained in 18 U.S.C. §2518(1) and discussed in text accompanying footnote 22.
90. The inventory requirement is contained in 18 U.S.C. §2518(8)(d) and discussed in text accompanying footnote 33.

XIV

Access

Can a person obtain access to United States government records?

Yes. The Freedom of Information Act (FOIA),[1] which was first passed in 1966 and substantially amended in 1974, allows a person to request and gain access to all records in the possession of agencies of the executive branch of the United States government except certain documents, or portions of documents, which fit within nine specified exemptions.[2] In addition, the Privacy Act [3] also allows people access to documents which pertain to themselves. The access provisions of the Privacy Act generally complement those in the FOIA.

The FOIA applies only to "agency records"—that is, records maintained by or under the control of an agency or department of the Executive branch, such as a cabinet department or the military.[4] The FOIA says that it is applicable to the Executive Office of the President, but the legislative history makes it clear that this provision was *not* meant to apply to the President's personal staff, whose sole function is to advise and assist the President. The FOIA also applies to government corporations or government-controlled corporations (such as the United States Postal Service, Amtrak, and the Federal Deposit Insurance Corporation). However, a corporation that is not chartered or controlled by the federal government is *not* subject to the FOIA simply because it receives federal funds. The FOIA does *not* apply to the records of state or local government,[5] private businesses, schools, organizations, or individuals.

The FOIA does not specifically define the meaning of a "record." However, in a 1967 memorandum interpreting the FOIA, then–Attorney General Ramsey Clark defined a "record" to include "all books, papers, maps, photographs, or other documentary materials, regardless of form or characteristics. . . ." On the other hand, he concluded that the FOIA does not include "structures, furniture, paintings, sculpture, three-dimension models, vehicles, equipment, etc., whatever their historical value or value 'as evidence.' " [6]

While the FOIA applies to all agency records, including but not limited to records about the requester, the Privacy Act authorizes access only to records about the requester. The Privacy Act applies to the same federal agencies as the FOIA and also to private contractors who operate a system of records for an agency to accomplish the agency's function.[7] This provision was designed to include within the scope of the Privacy Act records systems which are actually the agency's records, and which are used to accomplish an agency function, but which are operated by a private contractor. It does *not* apply to the records of all federal contractors. A business which contracts with the government for any purpose other than operating a records system is not subject to the Privacy Act.

The Privacy Act defines a *record* to mean

any item, collection, or grouping of information about an individual that is maintained by an agency, including, but not limited to, his education, financial transactions, medical history, and criminal or employment history and that contains his name, or the identifying number, symbol, or other identifying particular assigned to the individual, such as a finger or voice print or a photograph.[8]

Under this definition, a "record" can be as little as one descriptive item about a person, and it can be part of a larger document, record, or file.

What records are available for access by a requester?

The FOIA requires each agency to make certain information publicly available, even without a specific request. In addition, the FOIA gives a requester access to any agency records upon request, subject to the nine exemptions. The Privacy Act allows a requester access to personal records maintained by the agency in a system of records.[9]

The FOIA begins by requiring each agency to make two

categories of records absolutely available, without limitation by the exceptions. First, for the guidance of the public, the FOIA requires each agency to publish in the *Federal Register:*

1. description of the agency's organization, both in its central office and field offices;
2. descriptions of the procedures which have been established for obtaining access to agency records, including the places where records are located and the custodian of those records;
3. general descriptions of the agency's functioning and decision-making processes;
4. agency rules of procedure, description of agency forms along with the places at which such forms may be obtained, and instructions for all of the documents, reports or examinations required by the agency;
5. substantive rules of general applicability and statements of general policy formulated and adopted by the agency.[10]

The FOIA directs that a person shall not be bound by any rule, policy statement, or information that is required to be published in the *Federal Register* but which is not so published, unless that person is given "actual and timely notice of the terms thereof."

The FOIA provides that each agency must also make a second category of records available for public inspection and copying:

1. Final opinions made in the adjudication of particular administrative cases.
2. Any statements of policy and interpretations that have been adopted by the agency but not published in the *Federal Register*.
3. Administrative staff manuals that affect the public.
4. An index of the information required to be made public.[11]

An agency is authorized to delete personally identifying details contained in any of the above in order to prevent a clearly unwarranted invasion of personal privacy. Such deletions must be explained fully in writing.

In addition, the FOIA provides that "upon any request

for records" an agency "shall make the records promptly available to any person" if the requester reasonably describes the records and complies with applicable regulations.[12] Therefore, the requester does *not* have to show any relationship to, or special interest in, the documents requested; the requested documents do not have to be about the person making the request.[13]

The Privacy Act directs that each agency maintaining a system of records shall permit any individual to review or copy any record about that individual which is contained in the system. A *system of records* means a group of any records from which information is retrieved by the name of the individual or by some identifying number or symbol.[14] Thus, the definition of a system of records focuses on the method of retrieving information from the system: if retrieval is accomplished by reference to a personal identifier (e.g., name, Social Security number), then the system is subject to the Privacy Act. On the other hand, a records system organized by some means other than a personal identifier (e.g., Civil Service grade, date of employment with agency) is not subject to the Privacy Act. The Privacy Protection Study Commission (which was created by the Privacy Act to study information-privacy issues and recommend legislation) has pointed out that some agencies have purposely made their files retrievable by means other than personal identifiers in order to avoid the requirements of the Privacy Act.[15]

Can anybody obtain access to agency records?

Yes. The FOIA allows "any person" to request access to agency records.[16] Although not defined in the statute, a *person* has been interpreted to mean any individual, whether or not a citizen of the United States, as well as any business organization, association, or any other group of people.

The access provisions of the Privacy Act, however, are limited to an *individual,* defined as a "citizen of the United States or an alien lawfully admitted for permanent residence." [17] This provision was meant to exclude businesses and organizations. The Privacy Act was also meant to exclude the CIA and State Department files devoted solely to foreign nationals. The act provides that the parent of any minor or the legal guardian of any individual who has been declared to be incompetent may act on behalf of that individual.[18]

Can a person obtain access to documents without the help of a lawyer?

Yes. Both the FOIA and Privacy Act establish simple procedures for obtaining access to agency documents. It is not necessary to have a lawyer make a request for documents or to follow that request through the administrative process. Of course, if the requester later decides to bring a lawsuit challenging an agency decision, the assistance of a lawyer may be necessary.

How can a person obtain access to agency records?

A request for records can be in the form of a simple letter [19] to the head of the agency that controls or maintains the records.

The first step in requesting records is to identify the agency maintaining or controlling the desired records. In most instances this will not be difficult. People looking for personal records usually make a request to agencies with which they have had contact, such as agencies which have employed, served, or investigated the individual. A person who is not certain which agency has the desired records can write to the agencies likely to maintain relevant records. It may help to consult the *United States Government Organizational Manual*, which identifies and describes the functions of all federal agencies. The *Manual* is available in most libraries and may be purchased from the United States Government Printing Office in Washington, D.C.

A letter to the agency requesting access to personal records should begin by stating that the request is being made pursuant to the FOIA and the Privacy Act.[20] To speed processing, both the envelope and the letter should be clearly marked "FOIA/PA Request."

The FOIA requires that the requester "reasonably describe" the records requested. The legislative history of the FOIA suggests that this standard is satisfied if a professional employee of the agency, who is familiar with the subject area of the request, can locate the document without unreasonable effort. If a person wants documents pertaining to a particular subject, it is helpful to make the request as precise and limited as possible. The agency must advise you if it considers your request too vague to process. Generally, agency personnel will assist you in reformulating your request to conform to the applicable standards of specificity. If a person only wants documents pertaining to himself, it is usually sufficient to ask for "all records about me." Under the Privacy act there is usually not much difficulty describing the requested records because, as defined by the act, records are limited to personally identifiable information contained in a records system. It is therefore sufficient for the requester to ask for all information about himself.

For large agencies divided into many smaller units, the request should identify the particular departments having files. For example, if writing to the Justice Department, the requester should indicate if the request is for records maintained by the Criminal Division, Immigration and Naturalization Service, etc. It is permissible to ask for a search of the files of more than one department, but the requester may, instead, write separately to each department. Generally, a person seeking access to agency documents located in offices in different places should address a separate request to each location. For example, a person requesting FBI documents located in files both at headquarters in Washington, D.C., and in the Albany, New York office should address a separate request to each office.

The letter to the agency should also include your full name, address, and Social Security number. Many agencies require that your signature be notarized. All of this information is required so that the agency does not release information to people using false identification.

Finally, each agency is authorized to promulgate regulations governing the procedures for making FOIA and Privacy Act requests to that agency.[21] These regulations are available in the *Federal Register*. In addition, you may write to the agency itself for its regulations or simply ask for a copy of them in your request letter. If your request letter does not conform to the agency's regulations, the agency will respond by describing its defects and explaining how they may be corrected. In most instances, the agency personnel can be contacted directly for help in resolving any difficulties.

Does the government have to permit access to all requested agency records?

No. The FOIA contains nine exemptions which permit the agency to withhold information.[22] The Privacy Act also exempts certain agencies and categories of documents from its access provisions.[23]

The FOIA Exemptions

Exemption 1 allows the government to withhold information that has been *properly classified* pursuant to Executive Order. The applicable classification rules are contained in Executive Order 12065, which establishes both procedural and substantive requirements for classification, all of which must be satisfied before a document is properly classified and exempted under the FOIA. The minimum standard for classifying information—corresponding to the classification "confidential"—requires a determination that the unauthorized release of the information "could reasonably be expected to cause identifiable damage" to the "national defense or foreign relations of the United States." If the requester sues to obtain access to documents withheld under this exemption, the court must consider whether the documents were properly classified. However, the court is likely to give substantial weight to the agency's explanations unless the record is vague or the agency's claims suggest bad faith.

Exemption 2 exempts matters that are related solely to the *internal personnel rules and practices* of an agency. For the most part, this exemption applies only to minor or trivial matters not of genuine and significant public interest. The Supreme Court has recognized that Exemption 2 may be invoked to withhold matters of some public interest where necessary to prevent circumvention of agency regulations. Thus, for example, an agency may withhold investigative manuals used by the agency in its regulatory function.

Exemption 3 authorizes the withholding of matters *specifically exempted* from disclosure by another statute, but only if that other statute mandates withholding, establishes particular criteria, or refers to particular types of information. Congress has passed a number of statutes other than the FOIA which satisfy the prerequisites for this exemption. For example, laws governing the internal structure of the CIA, the secrecy of information pertaining to charges of employment discrimination, and the secrecy of Civil Aeronautics Board decisions pertaining to foreign-travel operations before submission to the President are all specifically mentioned in the legislative history of Exemption 3.[24] Statutes that merely *permit* the discretionary withholding of information are not sufficiently particular to satisfy the strict requirements of this exemption.

Exemption 4 exempts *trade secrets and privileged or confidential commercial or financial information.* A trade secret is generally defined as a "formula, patent device or compilation of information which is used in one's business and which gives [that person] an advantage over competitors who do not know it or use it." [25] A large body of law that has developed independent of the FOIA governs the application of this exemption. These matters usually arise only in commercial, rather than personal, FOIA cases. The second category of exempt information is confidential or privileged commercial or financial information obtained from a person. Commercial or financial information is considered to be confidential

> if disclosure of the information is likely to have either of the following effects: (1) to impair the government's ability to obtain necessary information in the future; or (2) to cause substantial harm to the competitive position of the person from whom the information was obtained." [26]

The requirement that the information be obtained from "a person" precludes the application of this exemption to information generated by the government.

Exemption 5 applies to information that would be *privileged in civil litigation* such as matters covered by the attorney-client privilege, the work-product privilege, and executive privilege. The *attorney-client* privilege covers confidential communications between attorney and client, and the *work-product* privilege covers material prepared in anticipation of litigation and for trial. Both privileges have had extensive comment and court consideration independent of the FOIA, and the application of this exemption requires reference to that body of law. The government alone can invoke an *executive* privilege for "materials reflecting deliberative or policy making processes" as opposed to "purely factual investigative matters."[27] The executive privilege is intended to insulate the deliberative process from public disclosure, thus encouraging uninhibited policy discussions. It generally applies only to predecision records.

Exemption 6 authorizes the agency to withhold *personnel and medical files* and "similar files the disclosure of which would constitute a clearly unwarranted invasion of personal privacy." The Supreme Court has said that the implementation of this exemption requires a balancing of the individual's expectation of privacy against the public benefits derived from opening agency action to public scrutiny. The statute's protection for only "clearly unwarranted" invasions of privacy has been interpreted to mean that the balance should be tilted in favor of disclosure.

Exemption 7 pertains to *investigatory records compiled for law-enforcement purposes,*

but only to the extent that the production of such records would

(A) interfere with enforcement proceedings,

(B) deprive a person of a right to a fair trial or impartial adjudication,

(C) constitute an unwarranted invasion of personal privacy,

(D) disclose the identity of a confidential source and, in the case of a record compiled by a criminal law enforcement authority in the course of a criminal investigation, or by an agency conducting a lawful national security intelligence investigation, confidential information furnished only by the confidential source,

(E) disclose investigative techniques and procedures, or

(F) endanger the life or physical safety of law enforcement personnel.[28]

Exemption 7 applies only to investigatory files compiled for law-enforcement purposes. In most instances, this would cover an individual's FBI files.

Exemption 8 protects records related to the examination,

operation, or condition of certain *financial institutions* subject to federal regulation.

Exemption 9 exempts *geological and geophysical* information and data.

Although the FOIA authorizes an agency to withhold information falling within the nine exempt categories, the statute does not *require* withholding; the government can release information even if it falls within the exemptions. Therefore, an individual desiring access to information should make the request even if it may appear to be exempt.

(See Chapter XII for Privacy Act exemptions.)

Can the agency charge any fees for providing access to documents?

Yes. The FOIA authorizes the government to charge both search fees and duplicating fees.[29] The Privacy Act authorizes only duplicating fees.[30]

Search fees pay for the cost of locating the requested documents; duplicating fees are the charges for copying them. Both the FOIA and the Privacy Act require the agencies to make regulations establishing reasonable standard fees.

Most agencies charge a standard search fee of $3.50 per hour. However, the Privacy Act, which pertains only to requests for personal records, does not authorize the government to charge any search fees. Therefore, although technically a request for personal records under the FOIA is subject to a charge for search fees, most agencies do not charge search fees for personal records. Most agencies charge a duplication fee of ten cents a page.

The FOIA also has a limited provision for fee waiver "where the agency determines that waiver or reduction of the fee is in the public interest because furnishing the information can be considered as primarily benefitting the general public." [31] Thus the statute empowers *the agency* to decide whether to waive the fee, and its decision is likely to be upheld by the courts unless it acts arbitrarily and inconsistently. Although an individual may have good reasons to want a fee waiver, such as poverty, the FOIA authorizes such a waiver only if the release of the requested information primarily benefits the public, rather than the individual. The general claim that the release of information benefits the public because it exposes government operations to public scrutiny and control has not been accepted by the agencies.

An agency is *not* permitted to charge for the time spent in reviewing requested documents and determining whether they may be released.

Is there any way to appeal an agency decision to withhold information?

Yes. The FOIA provides that if an agency denies any document, in whole or in part, the individual has a right to an administrative appeal.[32]

Under the FOIA, a letter telling the requester that all or part of the request has been denied must also tell of the right to appeal and say where the appeal should be directed. The person deciding the appeal must be the head of the agency or his designee, and must be superior to the employee responsible for the original denial.

A letter of appeal [33] should state clearly that it is made under the FOIA, state briefly what records are requested, and describe the original agency decision, including the dates of relevant correspondence. It may help to include a copy of the original request letter and the agency letter denying that request.

An appeal letter does *not* have to include arguments in support of the request for documents. It is sufficient merely to state that the original agency decision is appealed. The FOIA puts the burden on the government to sustain the decision not to release the records. Very often it is impossible to prepare a rebuttal on appeal because the agency gives the requester so little explanation of its rationale. However, if the requester does know why the agency is refusing to release the records and can identify specific arguments refuting the agency's contentions, it is worthwhile to include those arguments in the appeal letter.

Unlike the FOIA, the Privacy Act does not provide a right to administrative appeal. Many agencies nonetheless offer an appeal procedure employing the same mechanisms established for FOIA matters. If it denies the request, the agency will inform the requester of applicable procedures.

If the appeal process is available, it should be used in all cases in which the agency has not fully satisfied the request for documents. There are several reasons to appeal. First, the appeal may result in the release of additional records. Even though the appeal is within the same agency, it is decided by people other than those making the original decision; the appellate authority is often more distant from the records and has less of a proprietary interest in protecting them from release (this phenomenon is most evident in the Justice Department appellate review of FBI decisions). Second, the appeal is a simple process which does not require much investment of time or resources. Third, the appeal is an absolute prerequisite for bringing a court action to challenge the agency denial of an FOIA request.

If the appeal does not result in the release of all the requested records, the requester is entitled to challenge the agency denial in court.

Is the government required to respond promptly to requests for documents?

Yes. The FOIA provides that an agency must decide within ten working days after receipt of a request whether to comply.

It must then "immediately" notify the requester of the decision and the reasons.[34] If the requested records are denied, in whole or in part, the agency must advise the requester of the right to an appeal. If the requester appeals, the appeal must be decided within twenty working days after receipt by an agency.[35] If the decision is adverse the agency must advise of the right to judicial review.

In "unusual circumstances" the FOIA allows an agency to extend, for no more than ten working days, the period allowed for the initial determination and the period allowed for the appeal determination.[36] The act limits *unusual circumstances* to cases where the agency must (1) search for requested documents in field facilities or other offices, (2) search for and examine voluminous separate records demanded in a single request, or (3) consult with another agency having a substantial interest in the determination. If the agency invokes this provision, it must write to the requester, stating why the extension is needed and when the final determination is expected.

Unlike the FOIA, the Privacy Act does not require prompt response to a request for documents. However, implementing regulations prepared by the Office of Management and Budget (OMB) establish standards. Agencies should acknowledge requests within ten working days; whenever practicable, the agency should also decide whether access can be granted within those first ten working days, but in any event should decide and notify the requester in writing within thirty working days. If access is granted, the requester should receive the records within thirty working days; if, for good cause, the agency is unable to do so (for example, if the record is inactive and stored in a records center), it should inform the requester in writing that there will be a delay and how long it is expected to be.[87]

Despite the explicit time limits established by the FOIA, and the more lenient limits imposed by the Privacy Act regulations, the agencies rarely comply. Many agencies are deluged with requests and do not have the capacity for timely response. (Recently, the FBI was taking more than a year to respond to FOIA requests.) Except in emergencies, the requester has little alternative but to wait.

Can an agency be compelled to speed up the processing of an FOIA request?

In most instances, no. When an agency delays, the FOIA allows the requester to challenge the agency in court, but in most cases the court will stay the proceedings pending completion of the agency processing.

The FOIA provides that an agency's failure to respond within the statutory time period is a denial of the request.[38] Therefore, if an agency fails to respond within ten working days (or twenty days with an extension), the requester can proceed to the next step—appeal. If the agency fails to respond to the appeal within twenty days (or thirty days with an extension), then the requester can consider that delay a final denial and file a complaint in court challenging the agency's failure to release the records.

However, the act also provides that if such an action is begun, the court may stay the case to allow the agency to finish the administrative processing if "exceptional circumstances exist and the agency is exercising due diligence in responding to the request. . . ."[39] In at least one jurisdiction, courts have decided that the mere fact of an agency backlog of FOIA requests is sufficient to satisfy the "exceptional circumstances" test.[40] Even where the government must show exceptional circumstances and due diligence, courts have not usually required the government to comply with the time requirements of the FOIA, except in emergencies. If the requester has a special and urgent need for the records, the court may require the agency to process the records expeditiously. For example, if an individual is about to begin a criminal trial and the FOIA request is for documents necessary for the defense, the court may require the agency to accelerate the processing.[41]

Can a requester bring a lawsuit challenging an agency denial of requested records?

Yes. The FOIA and the Privacy Act authorize the United States district courts to reconsider an agency's decision to deny access to documents and to order the agency to produce records improperly withheld.

Before initiating a lawsuit, the requester must have made a request to an agency and been denied access to some or all of the documents sought. If the request is made under the FOIA, the requester must also have appealed the original denial and lost. If the agency fails to comply with applicable time limitations, the administrative remedies may be deemed exhausted without waiting for the agency's response.

Both the FOIA and Privacy Acts provide that the action may be filed either (1) where requester lives or (2) has a principal place of business, (3) where the records are located, or (4) in Washington, D.C.[42] FOIA cases "take precedence" over all other cases, except "cases the court considers of greater importance. . . ."[43]

In all FOIA and Privacy Act access cases, the requester-plaintiff has the advantage of a presumption that the records should be released. The government must overcome that presumption by demonstrating that the failure to release the records is justified.[44] The court may examine the disputed records *in camera*—that is, without the presence of the litigants—in order to determine if they should be released.[45]

The FOIA requires the release of *all* portions of documents not specifically subject to one of the nine exemptions.[46] Although the Privacy Act does not itself contain such a "segregability" provision, the OMB implementing guidelines provide that the record should be made available in the form in which it is maintained unless particular information with the record is properly withheld under the Privacy Act exemptions.[47] As a practical matter, an agency responding to a Privacy Act request deletes material in the same way as an agency responding to a FOIA request.

The Privacy Act requires that a suit to compel the agency to provide access to requested records must be brought "within two years from the date on which the cause of action arises."[48] Although this matter has not yet been firmly resolved, the cause of action for denying access should "arise" at the time of the final agency denial. Where an agency has materially and willfully misrepresented any information it is required to disclose and the misrepresented information is material to establishing the agency's liability to the individual under the Privacy Act, the action can be brought at any time within two years after the individual discovers the misrepresentation.

The FOIA, on the other hand, does not contain a statute-of-limitations provision.

Can the successful litigant recover attorney's fees and costs?

Yes. The FOIA and the Privacy Act authorize the court to assess reasonable attorney's fees and costs against the United States if the plaintiff has "substantially prevailed."[49] Under no circumstances may the government collect costs or attorney's fees from an unsuccessful plaintiff.

A plaintiff has "substantially prevailed" when he obtains a final judgment requiring the government to produce all requested records. The situation is less clear if the requester has won only a partial victory or if the requester has obtained the records, not because of a court decision but because the government has capitulated.

In determining whether the plaintiff has "substantially prevailed," the critical question is the extent to which the requester has obtained the records which the lawsuit originally sought to release. There is no formula for making these determinations. The court will look to the complaint, the documents, and the final resolution to determine if the plaintiff has prevailed to some substantial degree.

FOIA and Privacy Act cases are often resolved when the government voluntarily releases the documents after the start of litigation. It is now firmly established that a plaintiff may be able to recover attorney's fees and costs even if the government settles the case by releasing documents before final judgment.[50] However, some courts have been reluctant to award fees where it appears that the agencies would have released the documents even if the plaintiff did not file suit; this may occur when the lawsuit is filed before final agency processing is complete and the agency contends that the later release of the documents was the result of its own review and not the result of the lawsuit.

At least one appellate court considered two related factors, (1) whether the filing of the lawsuit could reasonably have been regarded as necessary, and (2) whether the lawsuit caused the agency to release the records.[51] The first consideration is designed to exclude the litigant who rushes into court immediately after the statutory time periods have passed without giving the agency the opportunity to finish its processing. Where the completion of the processing is long overdue and the agency has not given any firm commitment to complete the processing by a date certain, and where the delay in processing is not occasioned by a problem that can be promptly resolved, the initiation of the lawsuit is likely to be regarded as necessary. The second consideration is usually gauged by the surrounding circumstances. For example, the number of records released and the speed may be considered in determining whether the lawsuit caused the release of the records.

Even if the requester has substantially prevailed, the FOIA and the Privacy Act do not *require* the award of attorney's fees or costs. A court is more likely to award costs and attorney's fees if the request is in the public interest, if the requester has a particularly favored interest in the records (such as a scholar or journalist), or if the government did not have a reasonable basis to withhold the records. Courts are less likely to award fees and costs if the government had a reasonable basis to withhold or if the requester has a commercial interest in the records.

In most cases, a substantially prevailing plaintiff who has obtained access to personal records will be awarded attorney's fees and costs.

Some courts have held that a person appearing *pro se* (that is, representing himself without a lawyer's help) is entitled to attorney's fees.

Are there any provisions for penalizing a federal official who improperly withholds requested records?

Yes, but the FOIA penalty provision is extremely limited. The Privacy Act does not contain any penalty provision.

The FOIA provides that when a court orders the production of improperly withheld agency records and assesses attorney's fees and costs against the United States and, in addition, the court issues a written finding that the circumstances raise questions whether agency personnel acted arbitrarily or capriciously, the Civil Service Commission shall promptly initiate a proceeding to determine if disciplinary action is warranted.[52] The Commission shall investigate and submit its findings and recommendations to the administrative authority with responsibility for the agency, which shall take the corrective action recommended by the Commission. The penalty provision applies to all employees of agencies subject to the FOIA.

The penalty provision of the FOIA is not particularly strong. At most, it provides for an undefined administrative sanction, which can be imposed only after a series of conditions have been satisfied. The language of the statute suggests, and at least one lower court has held, that the penalty provision operates only if there is a court order requiring the production of agency records. Thus, unlike an award of attorney's fees and costs, the government may be able to avoid sanctions merely by disclosing the requested records before court judgment, even if the parties have been in litigation for a long while. Furthermore, even if a court orders production of records, it may be reluctant to issue written findings questioning whether agency personnel acted arbitrarily or capriciously.

The FOIA penalty provision has been only very rarely invoked, and there is no reason to believe that the threat of sanctions acts as a deterrent to arbitrary or capricious agency withholdings.

Can a person obtain access to state and local government records?

Perhaps, depending on the provisions of state and local laws and regulations.

The federal FOIA does not apply to state and local government records. However, most states have laws or regulations providing some access to government records. Many of the state statutes are patterned on the federal FOIA. However, there are many variations from state to state and it is beyond the scope of this book to detail them all.

A person desiring access to state and local government records may:

1. Seek the advice of a lawyer familiar with the state or local freedom-of-information law (many local bar associations will help people to contact a lawyer with the requisite skills).
2. Read the law—applicable state statutes can be found in all law libraries; many public libraries maintain a set of the state statutes.
3. Write to the state agency maintaining the requested records and simply request access. In most cases the agency will advise the requester if the request has failed to satisfy the procedures of the state law or if the requested records are exempt under state law. Of course, this process may result in delay but, for the requester who does not have access to information about the state statute, it may be the easiest first step.

NOTES

1. 5 U.S.C. §552.
2. The exemptions are described in 5 U.S.C. §552(b) and described in connection with the text accompanying footnote 22.
3. 5 U.S.C. §552a.
4. 5 U.S.C. §552(e).
5. In addition to the federal FOIA, many states have freedom-of-information laws that govern access to state and local government records.
6. Attorney General's Memorandum on the Public Infor-

mation Section of the Administrative Procedure Act [the FOIA], June 1967.

7. 5 U.S.C. §552a(m).
8. 5 U.S.C. §552a(a)(4).
9. 5 U.S.C. §552a(a)(5).
10. 5 U.S.C. §552(a)(1).
11. 5 U.S.C. §552(a)(2).
12. 5 U.S.C. §552(a)(3).
13. However, although a person cannot be denied access to documents *merely because* those documents are about another person, the information about another person may be deleted by the agency pursuant to exemptions protecting personal privacy. See exemptions 6 and 7(c), 5 U.S.C. §§552(b)(6) and (b)7(c) and text accompanying footnote 22.
14. 5 U.S.C. 552a(a)(5).
15. Privacy Protection Study Commission, Personal Privacy in an Informational Society 504 (1977).
16. 5 U.S.C. §552(a)(3).
17. 5 U.S.C. §552a(a)(2).
18. 5 U.S.C. §552a(h).
19. A sample request letter is included as Appendix A.
20. 5 U.S.C. §552(a)(3); 5 U.S.C. §552a(d).
21. 5 U.S.C. §552(a)(4)(A); 5 U.S.C. §552a(e)(4).
22. 5 U.S.C. §552(b).
23. 5 U.S.C. §552a(j) and (k).
24. 50 U.S.C. §403g, 42 U.S.C. §2000(e), and 49 U.S.C. §1461 respectively.
25. RESTATEMENT OF TORTS, §757, comment (b) (1939).
26. National Parks and Conservation Ass'n v. Morton, 498 F.2d 765, 770 (D.C.Cir. 1974).
27. EPA v. Mink, 410 U.S. 73, 89 (1973). *See generally* Dorsen and Shattuck, *Executive Privilege, the Congress and the Courts,* 35 OHIO ST. L. J. 1 (1974).
28. 5 U.S.C. §552(b)(7).
29. 5 U.S.C. §552(a)(4)(A).
30. 5 U.S.C. §552(a)(f)(5).
31. 5 U.S.C. §552(a)(4)(A).
32. 5 U.S.C. §552(a)(6)(A).
33. A sample letter of appeal is included as Appendix B.
34. 5 U.S.C. §552(a)(6)(A)(i).
35. 5 U.S.C. §552(a)(6)(A)(ii).
36. 5 U.S.C. §552(a)(6)(B).
37. Office of Management and Budget, *Privacy Act Guidelines,* §(d)(i) 40 Fed. Reg. 28,949, 28,958 (1975).
38. 5 U.S.C. §552(a)(6)(C).
39. 5 U.S.C. §552(a)(6)(C).

40. **Open America** v. Watergate Special Prosecution Force, 547 F.2d 605 (D.C.Cir. 1975).
41. Cleaver v. Kelley, 427 F.Supp. 80 (D. DC. 1976).
42. 5 U.S.C. §552(a)(4)(A); 5 U.S.C. §552a(g)(5).
43. 5 U.S.C. §552(a)(4)(D).
44. 5 U.S.C. §552(a)(4)(B); 5 U.S.C. §552a(g)(3)(A).
45. 5 U.S.C. §552(a)(4)(B); 5 U.S.C. §552a(g)(3)(A).
46. 5 U.S.C. §§552(a)(4)(B) and 552(b).
47. Office of Management and Budget, *Privacy Act Guidelines*, §(d)(1), 40 Fed. Reg., 28,949, 28,957 (1975).
48. 5 U.S.C. §552a(g)(5).
49. 5 U.S.C. §552(a)(4)(E); 5 U.S.C. §552a(g)(3)(B).
50. Vermont Low Income Advocacy Council v. Usery, 546 F.2d 509 (2d Cir. 1976).
51. *Id.*
52. 5 U.S.C. §552(a)(4)(F).

XV

Correction

Is there any way for a person to correct or amend agency records?

Yes. The Privacy Act requires that each agency maintaining a system of records shall permit a person to request amendment of a record pertaining to that individual.[1] (The Freedom of Information Act, however, contains only access provisions and does not afford an individual any right to correct or amend the information in the file.) This provision applies to all federal executive agencies, independent regulatory agencies, and private contractors that operate systems of records for any agency to accomplish an agency function.[2] It pertains only to records about the individual seeking the amendment and only if such a record is maintained in an agency system of records. A *system of records* means any group of records from which information is retrieved by reference to the name, or other identifying symbol, of the individual.[3] An *individual* is a United States citizen or a permanent resident alien.[4]

On what grounds may a person seek correction or amendment of agency records?

The Privacy Act requires that agencies maintain records that are accurate, relevant, timely, and complete.[5] A person may request amendment of any record which fails to satisfy one or more of those standards.[6] The act does not define the terms, but it provides some clues.

In describing the record-keeping requirements imposed on the federal agencies, the Privacy Act says they shall "maintain all records which are used by the agency in making any determination about any individual with such accuracy, relevance, timeliness and completeness, as is reasonably necessary to assure fairness to the individual in the determination." [7]

The meaning of *relevance* is somewhat further described by the requirement that each agency "maintain in its records only such information about an individual as is relevant and necessary to accomplish a purpose of the agency. . . ." [8] The "relevance" and the "completeness" standards, in conjunction, require that agencies eliminate all extraneous information, and, at the same time, include in the records all of the information necessary for their proper use.

"Accuracy" and "timeliness" are not defined. In some instances the issue will be the truth or falsity of an objective fact, e.g., the date of an event, the status of an employment relationship, or the disposition of an arrest. In other cases, accuracy will involve more subjective judgments, and will be more difficult to demonstrate. For example, the reason a person left a previous job may be perceived differently by the employee and the employer. Questions of "timeliness" involve similar subjective judgments. As with relevance, it seems appropriate to look to whether dated information is necessary to accomplish a purpose of the agency. Until these matters are settled in the courts, there are no generally applicable criteria to determine when a bit of information becomes too stale.

The provisions for amending records do not permit the alteration of evidence that has been presented in judicial or administrative proceedings. Any changes to such evidentiary records must be made according to the rules governing those proceedings. Similarly, the Privacy Act does not permit the individual to challenge information which has already been the subject of judicial or administrative action. For example, a person can not use the Privacy Act to challenge the accuracy of a conviction record on the grounds that the conviction was improper. However, a person could seek amendment of a record which improperly described the details of the conviction.

How does a person challenge the accuracy, relevancy, timeliness, or completeness of agency records?

The procedures for amending or expunging records are similar to the procedures for gaining access to records:

the individual must write to the agency, the agency will then process the request administratively, and the individual can obtain court review if the request is denied.

First, of course, a requester must obtain access to the agency records to see what they say.[9] When the agency sends those records, it should describe the procedures for challenging the records.

The Privacy Act requires each agency to establish procedures for reviewing a request from an individual concerning the amendment of a record, making a determination on that request for amendment, and providing for an appeal within the agency if there is an adverse determination.[10] The applicable procedures may be obtained from the agency itself, or may be found in the *Federal Register*.

Although the specific details may vary from agency to agency, the procedures are generally similar. The request for amendment should be made in writing, even though some agencies may permit an oral request in person or on the telephone. A written request will be important later in the amendment process if the request is denied. If a written request is inadequate in some respect, or fails to satisfy the agency prerequisites, the agency should advise the requester of the defects and how they can be corrected. To verify an individual's identity the agency may require an address, Social Security number, and notarized signature. It may save some time to include that information in the original request for amendment.

The letter to the agency should describe briefly the objectionable information, the grounds of the objection (the reason for believing the record is inaccurate, irrelevant, outdated, or incomplete) and the changes requested.

The Privacy Act requires that an amendment request must be acknowledged within ten working days and "promptly"[11] decided. Applicable regulations provide that the request for correction should also be decided, wherever practicable, within ten business days, so that the acknowledgment and the decision will be contained in one letter. In any event the amendment request should be completed "as soon as reasonably possible," normally within thirty working days from the receipt of the request.[12]

In deciding the correction request, the agency may, of course, simply make the correction as requested. Or it may refuse to amend the record, in which case it must

inform the individual of its refusal to amend the
record in accordance with his request, the reason for
the refusal, the procedures established by the agency
for the individual to request a review of that refusal
by the head of the agency or an officer designated by
the head of the agency, and the name and business
address of that official.[13]

Does a person have any recourse if a request for amendment is denied?

Yes. If a request for amendment is denied, the agency
must give the individual the right to appeal to the head of
the agency or his designee. In addition, the Privacy Act
allows a person denied an amendment to insert a concise
statement of disagreement in the record.

Unlike the access provisions of the Privacy Act, the
amendment provisions of the act require that when an
agency refuses to make a requested change the individual
must be given the right to appeal.[14] In its letter denying
the amendment request, the agency must describe the
procedures for appeal and the name of the individual to
whom that appeal should be directed. The appeal letter
should describe the original request and the initial agency
denial (it may help to enclose copies of the earlier correspondence) and ask that the original agency denial be
reviewed. If the individual has any additional reasons for
making the amendment, those reasons should be briefly
stated.

The Privacy Act requires that the agency must decide
the appeal within thirty business days from the date the
review is requested. The head of the agency may extend
that deadline by an additional thirty days if there is "good
cause shown." [15] If the appeal is denied, the appeals
officer must state, in writing, the reasons and must advise
the requester of the right to file a statement of disagreement and the right to judicial review.

If the agency denies a request for amendment, it must
permit the individual to file with the agency a concise
statement setting forth the reasons for disagreement.[16] In
response, if the agency deems it appropriate, it may also
include in the record a concise statement of the agency's

reasons for not making the requested amendments. The statement of disagreement must be provided to anyone to whom the disputed information is subsequently disclosed.

Can a person bring a lawsuit to compel the agency to make the requested amendment?

Yes. The Privacy Act provides that whenever an agency makes a determination not to amend an individual's record, the United States district courts shall have jurisdiction to determine the controversy.[17] The court may order the agency to amend the record in accordance with the request or in another way.

Before bringing a lawsuit, the individual must exhaust all administrative remedies—that is, the initial request and appeal must have been denied. As with an access lawsuit, a lawsuit to correct may be filed in the district where the individual resides or has a principal place of business, where the agency records are kept, or in the District of Columbia.[18]

An individual must bring a lawsuit within two years after the cause of action arises (when the agency finally denies the request for amendment) or, if an agency has misrepresented information that is material to establishing the agency's liability, within two years after discovery of the misrepresentation.[19]

In an amendment lawsuit, the Privacy Act does *not* specify whether the individual has the principal burden of convincing the court that the agency's decision was wrong, or whether the government must bear the burden of establishing that its decision was correct. This issue— which party has the burden of proof—is yet to be resolved by the courts. The regulations of the OMB note that the burden was not expressly placed on the agency and concludes that the omission was "intended to result in placing the burden of challenging the accuracy of the record upon the individual." [20]

The Privacy Act does clearly provide that the court may assess costs and attorney's fees against the United States if the requester "substantially prevails." [21] The attorney's fees and costs provision of the Privacy Act are identical to the corresponding provisions of the FOIA and are likely to be subject to similar interpretations.[22]

Are any agency records exempt from the Privacy Act amendment provisions?

Yes. The agency records that are excluded from operation of the Privacy Act *access* provisions are also excluded from the amendment provisions. These Privacy Act exemptions are described in Chapter XIV.[23] Although the amendment provisions of the Privacy Act do not apply to records maintained by many important agencies (such as the CIA, the Secret Service, and in most instances, the FBI), records of most social-service and personnel agencies (e.g., the Department of Health, Education, and Welfare and the Civil Service Commission) are subject to the amendment provisions.

Does an agency have to correct inaccuracies in records that were disseminated before the record was amended?

Yes. If an agency amends a record in compliance with a request or order, it must notify prior recipients of that record of the changes. If the prior recipients are other federal agencies, they must also correct their records.[24]

Similarly, if the record is not amended, and the individual files a statement of disagreement, that statement must be sent to prior recipients of the record.[25]

The agency's duty to notify prior recipients is tied to its obligation, under the Privacy Act, to keep an accounting of its disclosures of personal records to other agencies or individuals.[26] This requirement excludes disclosures to employees of the agency having a need to know the information or disclosures made pursuant to the Freedom of Information Act. However, the obligation to maintain such an accounting was first imposed only when the Privacy Act became effective on September 27, 1975. Therefore, even if a record is amended or a statement of disagreement is filed, the agency will not be able to identify agencies or individuals that may have received the records before then.

NOTES

1. 5 U.S.C. §552a(d)(2).
2. 5 U.S.C. §552a(a)(1) and (m).
3. 5 U.S.C. §552a(a)(5).

4. 5 U.S.C. §552a(a)(2).
5. 5 U.S.C. §552a(e)(5).
6. 5 U.S.C. §552a(d)(2).
7. 5 U.S.C. §552a(e)(5).
8. 5 U.S.C. §552a(e)(1).
9. The procedures for obtaining access to documents are explained in Chapter XIV.
10. 5 U.S.C. §552a(f)(4).
11. 5 U.S.C. §552a(d)(2)(B).
12. Office of Management and Budget, *Privacy Act Guidelines* §(d)(2)(A), 40 Fed. Reg. 28,949, 28,958 (1975).
13. 5 U.S.C. §552a(d)(2)(B)(ii).
14. 5 U.S.C. §552a(d)(3).
15. *Id.*
16. *Id.*
17. 5 U.S.C. §552a(g)(2).
18. 5 U.S.C. §552a(g)(5).
19. 5 U.S.C. §552a(g)(5).
20. 5 U.S.C. §552a(g)(5).
21. U.S.C. §552a(g)(3)(B).
22. See Chapter XIV.
23. 5 U.S.C. §552a(j) and (k); see discussion of exemptions in text accompanying Chapter XIV, footnote 23.
24. 5 U.S.C. §552a(c)(4).
25. *Id.*
26. 5 U.S.C. §552a(c).

Appendix A

SAMPLE REQUEST LETTER

> Your address
> Your telephone no.
> Date

Director
United States Agency
Washington, D.C.

Dear Madam/Sir,
  This is a request under the Freedom of
Information Act (5 U.S.C. §552) and the
Privacy Act (5 U.S.C. §552a). I request a
copy of [describe your request; for
example "all documents maintained by
your agency about me"].

  In the event that you determine that
some portion of a file is exempt from
release, I request that you release any
reasonably segregable portion of the
documents which is not exempt. I, of
course, reserve my right to appeal such
decisions.

  In addition, if you determine that some
or all of the report is exempt, I request
that you advise me of the applicable
exemption and explain why it applies in
this case.

  As you know, the law permits you to waive
or reduce fees if that is "in the public
interest because furnishing the informa-

tion can be considered as primarily benefitting the public." I believe that this request fits that category and ask you to waive any fees.

If you have any questions regarding this request, please feel free to contact me.

Sincerely,

Your name

Appendix B

SAMPLE APPEAL LETTER

Your address
Your telephone no.
Date

Secretary of Department
United States Department
Washington, D.C.

Dear Madam/Sir:
This is an appeal pursuant to the Freedom Of Information Act (5 U.S.C. §552).

On —— I received a letter from —— of your Department advising me that my request for access to documents has been denied in part. I am enclosing a copy of my exchange of correspondence with your agency so that you can see what files I have requested and that the request has been denied.

I trust that upon examination of my request you will conclude that the information sought is not properly covered by the exemptions cited. I expect that you will make such information available promptly.

If you are unable to order release of the requested information, I intend to initiate a lawsuit to compel its disclosure.

                Sincerely,

                Your name

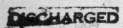

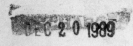